Gamaliel Painter

ALSO BY STORRS LEE

Father Went to College, Wilson-Erickson, 1936.

(Editor) *Bread Loaf Anthology*, Middlebury College Press, 1939.

Stage Coach North, Macmillan, 1941.

(Editor) *Footpath in the Wilderness*, Middlebury College Press, 1942.

Town Father: A Biography of Gamaliel Painter, Hasting House, 1952.

Green Mountains of Vermont, Holt, 1955.

Yankees of Connecticut, Holt, 1957.

The Strength to Move a Mountain, Putnam, 1958.

God Bless Our Queer Old Dean, Putnam, 1959.

Canal Across a Continent, Harrap, 1961.

The Sierra, Putnam, 1962.

The Great California Deserts, Putnam, 1963.

(Contributor) *A Vanishing America*, Holt, 1964.

The Islands, Holt, 1966.

(Editor) *Partridge in a Swamp: Journals of Viola C. White*, Countryman Press, 1979.

Editor of "Literary Chronicle" series, published by Funk:

Hawaii: A Literary Chronicle, 1967.

Maine: . . ., 1968.

California: . . ., 1968.

Washington State: . . ., 1969.

Colorado: . . ., 1970.

Gamaliel Painter

W. Storrs Lee

With an Introduction by John M. McCardell Jr.

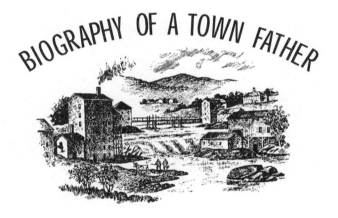

BIOGRAPHY OF A TOWN FATHER

Drawings by Edward Sanborn

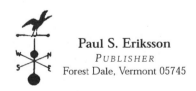

Paul S. Eriksson
PUBLISHER
Forest Dale, Vermont 05745

Printed in the United States of America.

4 3 2 1

First issued in 1952 by Hastings House under the title *Town Father.*
Reprinted by permission of the author.

Library of Congress Cataloging-in-Publication Data

Lee, W. Storrs (William Storrs), 1906-
    [Town father]
    Gamaliel Painter : biography of a town father / by W. Storrs Lee; introduction
by John M. McCardell, Jr.
      p. cm.
    Originally published: Town father. New York ; Hastings House, 1952. With
new introd.
    Includes bibliographical references and index.
    ISBN 0-8397-2343-1
    1. Painter, Gamaliel, 1743-1819. 2. Pioneers--Vermont--Middlebury--
Biography. 3. Legislators--Vermont--Biography. 4. Businessmen--Vermont--
Biography. 5. Middlebury (Vt.)--History. 6. Middlebury College--History.
7. Middlebury (Vt.)--Biography. 8. Middlebury College--Biography. I. Title.

F59.M6L.42 2001
974.3'503'092--dc21
   [B]   2001023922

Photo of Gamaliel Painter: Courtesy of Henry Sheldon Museum of Vermont History

CONTENTS

FOUNDERS AND A FOUNDER, vii

INTRODUCTION BY JOHN M. MCCARDELL, JR., xi

    1 *Pioneer,* 3

    2 *Rebel,* 25

    3 *Artificer,* 53

    4 *Farmer,* 79

    5 *Sheriff,* 97

    6 *Judge,* 113

    7 *Industrialist,* 131

    8 *Educator,* 151

    9 *Churchman,* 169

   10 *Legislator,* 183

   11 *Civil Engineer,* 203

   12 *Philanthropist,* 219

REFERENCE SOURCES, 239

ABOUT THE AUTHOR, 245

INDEX, 247

TO
MARY LOU

FOUNDERS AND A FOUNDER

All American towns with a Colonial infancy or adolescence had their Gamaliel Painters. Very few had founding fathers whose names became as familiar as Thomas Hooker, Roger Williams or William Penn, but destiny tapped all of them as grandsires of communities; each had a common cut and character. With obstinacy, confidence, and frequently with wisdom, they went about their job, struggling against conflicting ideologies, the elements, their neighbors. Always the Gamaliel Painters met with persistent hardship; almost always they met with success, and lived to be honored with deference proportionate to their doings, finally were given a grand burial, and a bulky gravestone. A street, a building, an institution or a park was eventually named for them, if they had not already managed to have themselves memorialized in the titles of the towns they had founded. When the time came, railroad conductors carried on from there with the task of perpetuation, calling out to an unheeding public: Brownington, Wheelock Bend, Brewster Corners, Belchertown, Dixfield, Sterlingford, Glastonbury, Montgomery Center, Starksboro.

The founders of the big towns became heroes to seventh grade history classes, and a valuable source of revenue to professional biographers. But the founders of the little towns stayed put in their graves, even though they were the makers of America. After a generation or two they were forgotten unless some jocular incident or shortcoming was resurrected and attached to them in the form of a tradition.

Gamaliel Painter was the principal founder of Middlebury, a little college town in central Vermont. He was more ingenious than great, more resolute than noble. He was typical of the many scores of men in the sixteen and seventeen hundreds who built towns on sheer persistence, patience and prayer. Like the founders of the other little towns, he was given a magnificent burial and a fine tombstone. A park was named for him; a college building was named for him; a professorship was named for him. But through the years, the park began to be called something else and a Professorship of Natural Philosophy was no longer needed. Students living in a dormitory had to have an address, so his name stuck to Painter Hall, though few freshmen ever bothered to inquire what Painter's first name was, or who he was. Undergraduates who became inquisitive about the portrait of a stubborn-looking character eyeing the students of Rhetoric and English Literature were told by the professor that it was supposed to be Gamaliel Painter who built Painter Hall.

Then in 1916 interest in Gamaliel was suddenly awakened. A cane, said to be one the founder carried, was unearthed in the college museum, dusted off, properly engraved and put to use. The College needed a colorful symbol. An edict was issued that hereafter the cane would be displayed in the hands of the President only after an athletic victory over Middlebury's irrepressible rival—the University of Vermont. Following a defeat it would disappear into mysterious and sacred seclusion. The idea was so contagious that it blossomed into an age-old tradition in less than a year.

Gamaliel Painter lived again. His future was secure. A song was written about him and his cane; football teams conquered in its courage; under emotional stress students pledged themselves "to do as Painter did"; in their choruses the fraternity boys interspersed rappings and tappings to simulate Painter's hobbling with his staff; the senior women came out with replicas of the cane and introduced a commencement ceremony as colorful as a West Point wedding; grown alumni reverently rose to their feet, doffed their hats and held them over their hearts while they sang of Gamaliel. The song was published in university collections and sung on other campuses. Audiences in Carnegie Hall and Symphony Hall applauded glee club renditions of "Gamaliel Painter's Cane," and judicious music critics commended the song and the singing. The cane brought Painter more recognition than he had suffered in his entire life.

Then people began to be curious about who this man was that they were singing about, and it was discovered that no one knew very much. In his day Middleburians knew all about him. They knew so much about him that it was superfluous to put it on paper for the benefit of those who knew the same. No one had considered it necessary to organize biographical notes until it was too late—until most of his contemporaries were in graves adjacent to his. To local historians he passed on a wealth of information about others, but he was chary of furnishing information about himself.

Painter was as slow at writing as he was slow of speech. He

was too canny to commit himself on any but the safest issues. If he kept a diary, he apparently saw to it that it was disposed of; if he kept a file of correspondence, he did not intentionally permit samples of it to get into the hands of the public. He may have had good reasons for not wanting to expose to public scrutiny the evidence of some of his transactions, and his diffidence made a secret of his greater virtues. In preparing his biography it was therefore occasionally necessary to cement facts with circumstantial evidence where church and town records fail, where state and military records present gaps. If Painter and his contemporaries had deliberately contrived to conceal his story they would scarcely have made the recounting more difficult. He had the major role in creating a town and a college. Without his efforts neither would have come of age.

To Mr. Eugene Tilleux of Arlington, Virginia, an expression of deep gratitude is due for his very generous and scholarly assistance in checking, transcribing and interpreting a vast assortment of details related to Painter and the Revolutionary artificers in the Library of Congress, State Department and military archives in Washington, D.C. Without his tenacious and enthusiastic support, many of the gaps in the biography would never have been filled.

INTRODUCTION

By John M. McCardell, Jr., President, Middlebury College

Since its founding in 1800, Middlebury has uniquely been known as "the Town's College," an association reinforced by David Stameshkin, who gave his first volume of the College's history this most appropriate title. In this our Bicentennial year we have been reminded in so many ways that Middlebury, Town and College, bear the same name, share the same history, and together face a challenging future.

Middlebury College was the product of a vision shared by a group of townspeople who, in the 1790s, believed fervently that an institution of higher education would forever set their community apart and bring it stature and prosperity. Foremost among these leaders were Seth Storrs, on whose land, now known as Storrs Park, the Addison County Grammar School, forerunner of Middlebury College, was built, and Gamaliel Painter, in whose mind burned so brightly the vision of a future he could not describe very articulately or in much detail, but which he was determined to pursue. These men and their colleagues first met with Timothy Dwight, President of Yale, in 1798, and then on November 1, 1800, secured a charter for Middlebury College. On November 4, 1800, the College, occupying the Addison County Grammar School building, opened its doors to students.

The institution thus established might properly have borne the name of Storrs or Painter. But, unlike most other institutions founded during this time, it instead was named not for a person but for a place. From the beginning, then, Middlebury College understood itself to be a part of a community that extended beyond its own immediate boundaries. In 1800 those limits did not reach beyond the Village line; by 2000 the reach of Middlebury College was global. Yet throughout its history, the College has never forgotten how it began and has never seriously thought its name should be other than that of the town that gave it birth.

The founding generation did not leave much of an historical record behind. And so little beyond their names was known of Painter or Storrs or their associates until the discovery of Gamaliel Painter's cane in 1916 awakened a new interest in this town father. Young W. Storrs Lee '28 sang the well known song, "Gamaliel Painter's Cane," as an undergraduate and determined to learn more about this distant, mysterious founder. The pages that follow are the results of his prodigious research. First published in 1952 with the title Town Father, Lee's work imaginatively recreated the life of Gamaliel Painter and added detail to the bare outlines of his life and achievements. Though from afar, Storrs Lee has remained one of the loyal champions of his alma mater for more than 60 years. With the present volume, Middlebury College extends its thanks to him and welcomes him home.

It may very well be that the discovery of the cane, the composition of the song, the publication of this biography, and the later restoration of the Painter House by Middlebury College has given Gamaliel Painter undue prominence in the annals of early nineteenth century Middlebury. If undue, it would certainly not

xii

be the sort of prominence he sought. But battles over ranking are best left to the academic arena. There can be no question that the story of the life of Gamaliel Painter is intrinsically interesting as told by Storrs Lee and thus offers valuable insights into that distant past that shaped so much of what our college is today. Nor can there be any doubt that Painter has inspired in generations of Middlebury students a special kind of loyalty to alma mater. His story merits telling, and re-telling.

And thus with gratitude I welcome the republication of this volume and thank both Paul Eriksson '40 and Storrs Lee himself in arranging for its reissue and inviting me to prepare this introduction. Looming large over our history, staring down at us from his austere portrait, and coming to life in these pages, Gamaliel Painter sets a stern and worthy example. As we enter a new century and a new millennium, his life reminds us of those who came before us, who created the institution that has now passed into our own temporary custody, and from whom we take confidence, courage, and hope as we seek to follow their examples and transmit to our own successors a college that is true to its past and ever seeking to become a stronger and better version of itself.

Gamaliel Painter

1 PIONEER

They were the pick of northern Connecticut malcontents. They were speculators and escapists. A few of them were idealists. They were adventurers intent on getting a little further away from the reach of probing British sovereignty, men with obsessions for community independence and personal independence, men with a lust for space, unbroken horizons and a bargain, even a poor bargain. They were resourceful but impecunious, ready to purchase a change of address with the currency of hard labor, grim discomfort and warm lead as long as freedom from restraint went with the purchase.

Returning from the final conquest of Canada in 1760, scores of infantrymen had broken ranks to make exploratory detours

3

through the Champlain Valley in New Hampshire. They liked the looks of the country and the feel of the soil. Many had even picked tentative home sites. From the wars they had returned to areas like Litchfield County in Connecticut and passed the word to their neighbors in Salisbury, Sharon, Cornwall, Canaan, that the broad forest land east of Lake Champlain was the promised land of New England. Moreover it was being advertised by the Governor of New Hampshire on a come-and-get-it basis; given a suitable number of pioneer proprietors, one had only to survey a future town, identify it, charter it, pay a nominal fee of twenty pounds and occupy it.

The Litchfield speculators and malcontents, the idealists and escapists, recognized the easy bargain, formed a corporation, and packed off John Everts and Elias Reed to do the surveying. Everts and Reed were two of their kind, masters of backwoods diplomacy, devoted to the cause of escape from authority. John was commissioned to plot out two towns, Elias one. With a *carte blanche* commission they tramped north— far north of Bennington where the good sites were already spoken for, north of Manchester where settlement was in the making, north even of Rutland and Pittsford where the last signs of civilization ceased to exist and the military cart paths turned west to New York rather than venture further into the Green Mountain wilderness.

They found an area which apparently no prospector had previously dared stake off, and Everts was so taken with the country that he eagerly plotted three towns instead of two. Together they mapped and marked a magnificent tract of over a hundred thousand acres, stretching clear across the Valley from Lake Champlain to the Green Mountains, a vast forest of pine, hemlock, maple, oak, cut through the middle by a

4

meandering stream which French explorers a century before had labeled the Creek of Otters.

They returned to Salisbury, Connecticut, where the idealists and adventurers, the escapists and speculators readily subscribed for plots of a hundred acres, two hundred acres, three hundred acres. The surveys and signatures were hurried to Governor Wentworth, and the agents brought back the Charters from Portsmouth for four wilderness towns in New Hampshire sentimentally named after their own Connecticut towns: Salisbury, New Haven, Cornwall and Middlebury.

All together there were some two hundred signatories who affixed their names as proprietors to the corporate venture of founding four towns, but once the charters were in their hands, the corporation was divided four ways, dissolved, and warnings for four separate town meetings posted. Middlebury held its first meeting one wintry morning, the fifth of January, 1762, at Salisbury, Connecticut. It was called to order in John Everts' rustic tavern, and there in the homely informality lent by kettles, spinning wheels and hanging shanks of dried beef, the savor of the chartered document was revealed:

PROVINCE OF NEW HAMPSHIRE

GEORGE THE THIRD, BY THE GRACE OF GOD, OF GREAT BRITAIN, FRANCE AND IRELAND, KING, DEFENDER OF THE FAITH, &C.

To All Persons to Whom These Presents shall come,

GREETING

Know Ye, that we of our special grace, certain knowledge and mere motion, for the due encouragement of settling a new Plantation within our said Province, by and with the advice of our trusty and well-beloved Benning Wentworth, Esq., our Governor and Commander in Chief of our said Province of New Hampshire . . . do give and grant in equal

5

shares, unto our loving subjects . . . whose names are entered on this Grant, to be divided to, and amongst them into sixty-eight equal shares, all that tract or parcel of land situate, lying and being within our Province of New Hampshire, containing by admeasurement 25,040 acres, which tract is to contain something more than six miles square, and no more; . . . butted and bounded as follows, viz: beginning at the southerly corner of a township granted this day by the name of New Haven, at a tree marked, standing on the bank of the easterly or northeasterly side of Otter Creek so called, from thence running east seven miles then turning off and running south ten degrees west, six miles and sixty-four rods, then turning off and running west to Otter Creek aforesaid; then down said creek, as that runs to the bound first mentioned . . . ; to have and to hold the said tract of land as above expressed, together with all the privileges and appurtenances, to them and their respective heirs and assigns forever, upon the following conditions, viz:

I. That every Grantee, his heirs or assigns shall plant and cultivate five acres of land within the term of five years for every fifty acres contained in his or their share or proportion of land in said township . . . on penalty of the forfeiture of his Grant. . . .

II. That all white and other pine trees . . . fit for masting our royal navy, be carefully preserved for that use . . .

III. That . . . a tract of land . . . near the centre of the said township . . . shall be reserved and marked out for town lots, one of which shall be allotted to each Grantee of the contents of one acre.

IV. . . . Rent of one ear of Indian corn only, on the twenty-fifth day of December annually . . .

V. Every proprietor . . . shall yield and pay . . . every year forever, from and after the expiration of ten years . . . one shilling Proclamation money for every hundred acres he so owns, settles or possesses . . . in our Council Chamber in Portsmouth.

In testimony whereof we have caused the seal of our said Province to be hereunto affixed. Witness Benning Wentworth, Esq., our Governor and Commander in Chief of our said Province, the second day of November in the year of our Lord Christ, one thousand seven hundred and sixty-one, and in the second year of our reign.

B. WENTWORTH.

Gamaliel Painter had no franchise at that first Middlebury town meeting. His name was not on the check list of proprietors. He was only nineteen, reticent and inarticulate, but his blustering brother Elisha, six years his senior, could more than make up for Gamaliel's reservation and argue the interests of both. The two were so opposite in trait, talent and character that no one unfamiliar with their background was readily persuaded that they belonged to the same family. And there were moments when Gamaliel was not particularly proud of the relationship, moments when Elisha's aggressive nature brought both of them embarrassment, and his surly swagger brought ostracism. Ever since the brothers had broken away from the family in New Haven, Elisha had served as the spokesman and Gamaliel, because he was a boy, and because his speech was faltering, lived under the spell of the domineering elder.

Neither was over-sentimental about family affiliation, but in a general way any Painter recognized responsibility when he saw it. Elisha was wise enough to the ways of the world to realize that the ruffian associates, like Ethan Allen, he had picked for himself were not the best moral benefactors for his younger brother. He insisted on giving Gamaliel the kind of gruff protection a grizzly might give to a half-grown cub, keeping him in the background, knowing that a youngster in his upper teens, despite his natural reserve, might take to their hearty spirit with too much self-assurance. But Gamaliel would soon be out of his teens and on his own. Although

7

Elisha himself had no consuming interest in settling permanently in the New Hampshire Grants, a lot there could provide a wholesome environment where Gamaliel might find himself, away from the Salisbury influences, and it would be a good investment in any case.

With all their differences Gamaliel and Elisha were typical of the men crowded into John Everts' tavern for the town meeting—mostly young men in farm boots, leathern jackets, and rough homespun trousers, unshaven and unsheared, careless of manner, oblivious of anything remotely related to refinement or dignity. They sat uneasily on the logs next to the cavernous fireplace, lined themselves self-consciously along the table benches, sat back to back on the solid trestle table, elbowed into doorways, and fumbled idly with the butter churn and farm tools left about the common room. Adventure was in their blood, adventure, restlessness and non-conformity. Like the Painters, their families had never managed to settle in one place for long.

Since the early 1600's the Painters had roved over southern New England from town to town, usually living in not the best seacoast society of Hingham, Charlestown, Westerley, Newport, New Haven. Even John Winthrop had taken the trouble to deplore the vagrancy of Gamaliel's great-great-grandfather Thomas, of whom he wrote scathingly: "A poor man of Hingham, one Painter, who had lived at New Haven and at Rowley and Charlestown, and been scandalous and burdensome by his idle and troublesome behavior to them all, was now on the sudden turned Anabaptist, and having a child born, he would not suffer his wife to bring it to the ordinance of baptism, for she was a member of the church, though himself were not. Being presented for this and enjoined to suffer the child to be baptised, he still refusing, and

8

disturbing the church, he was again brought to the court not only for his former contempt, but also for saying that our baptism was anti-christian; and in the open court he affirmed the same. Whereupon after much patience and clear conviction of his error, etc., because he was very poor, so as no other but corporal punishment could be fastened upon him, he was ordered to be whipped, not for his opinion, but for reproaching the Lord's ordinance, and for his bold and evil behavior both at home and in the court. He endured his punishment with much obstinacy, and when he was loosed, he said boastingly that God had marvelously assisted him. Whereupon two or three honest men, his neighbors, affirmed before all the company, that he was of very loose behavior at home, and given much to lying and idleness."

Gamaliel's great-grandfather Shubael had perpetuated the family trait and accumulated a record of considerable proportions with Rhode Island constabulary for contempt of authority, for "takeing Sheep ffeloniously," for selling his wife's property to which he did not have a clear title, and "for living with Hannah, the wife of Thomas Martin, contrary to law." Shubael knew the feel and the indignity of the stocks.

Grandfather Thomas had cut out a rough career for himself with the British regulars and had risen to the rank of Ensign, and Gamaliel's father had settled somewhat more respectably in Westhaven where he brought up the unruly family of three sons and as many daughters. But the family traits still came to the surface. Gamaliel's oldest brother had taken his wanderlust to sea and been lost in a hurricane. Elisha and Gamaliel, profiting by the lesson, were the first confirmed landlubbers in five generations and had headed inland to the Berkshire frontier.

Out of the miscellany of family virtues, Gamaliel had re-

tained a stubbornness, an aversion to domesticity, and a subdued interest in adventure. Quite inexplicably he had
acquired a spirit of caution that had seldom manifested itself
on his father's side of the family. He lived in the shadow of
his brother, was naturally backward in any indoor company
and was not even at home in the confinement of John Everts'
tavern, crowded though it was by his friends and companions.
Nor was he completely prepared for the kind of town meeting
that had developed. He had expected a few forceful speeches,
warnings from the conservatives on the dangers of the forest
north of Massachusetts, sober deliberation over candidates
for office, perhaps a substantial prayer or two.

But instead of an orderly meeting such as might have been
held in the town hall, this was more like a gathering of the
village ruffians. There was less drinking but not much more
emphasis on disciplined procedure. After the reading of the
charter, occasionally interrupted by unflattering remarks directed at their benefactors, His Excellency Benning Wentworth and His Majesty George III, they settled down to the
business of electing a town clerk, three selectmen, and a tax
collector, and to consideration of major matters of minor
finance. To Gamaliel it seemed that every detail of creating
a new town should be treated with seriousness and deliberation; individually they were all rebels of a sort, but it was one
thing to take an imposed authority lightly, quite another to
take efforts at forming their own government lightly. It was
the half-hearted interest in the venture that disturbed him
most, as if few of them really had serious intention of doing
anything about their grants for a long time. He knew these
men and knew when their intentions were genuine. Young,
naive, and logical, he failed to see the humor they saw in

appointing selectmen for a town that hadn't so much as a hut in it. No one had explained to him that there might be land speculators with mercenary interests among them. Of course the territory was not settled, but the election of town officers was at least a necessary step to organization. They were realists and so was he; they maintained that until someone was ready to fell trees, survey roads, and build homes, there was no need for ordered government; he saw government as a way of getting trees cleared and roads marked. Their immediate enthusiasm was to see the meeting over so that they could turn to the more pressing obligation to dispose of John Everts' modest supply of grog.

Gamaliel had to continue dreaming about a well-ordered community in New Hampshire for a far longer time than even the lightheartedness at the first meeting indicated. Month after month there was delay and procrastination, and the months extended into years. During those months he learned to distinguish between the sincerity of a prospective settler and the artifice of a speculator; in fact, he picked up for himself some rather practical notions on the potential returns from land speculation. At subsequent town meetings little more was accomplished than at the first. The lack of enthusiasm became contagious, and Gamaliel even raised little objection when Elisha proposed selling his speculative stake in New Hampshire to their neighbor, John Chipman. It was evident that Gamaliel could readily and cheaply secure a tract of land from another of the disinterested proprietors if he ever decided to migrate north. Elisha sold their holdings; and with the sale went Gamaliel's immediate interest in Middlebury.

The brothers moved into a small farm at Furnace Village in the southern end of Salisbury next to the iron foundry, with a doctor and a parson as their principal neighbors. When Elisha bought the farm in 1763, a tannery and roadside cobbler's shop went with the place, and Gamaliel began to learn something of the craft of shoemaking and tanning along with farming. Belatedly he devoted more time to his three R's and, as he got deeper into mathematics, he turned apprentice to a local surveyor and became thoroughly competent with his compass and chains. He had more amateur interests than he could cope with in Salisbury without speculating in Green Mountain territory.

By 1767, nearly five years after the first town meeting, he had become too preoccupied to accompany fifteen prospectors on an exploratory trip of Champlain Valley far north of Middlebury. But John Chipman was anxious to see the land he had just bought from Elisha. He was more concerned than anyone else about the possible loss of his grant if he did not fulfill the letter of their charter contract to the extent of clearing five out of every fifty acres within five years. Chipman took his obligations seriously, accompanied the expedition as far as the Middlebury-Salisbury line, and spent the summer cutting and burning some seven or eight acres along the shore of Otter Creek.

But by autumn when John brought back his enthusiastic report of the farming prospects in Middlebury, Gamaliel had bought out his brother—farm, tannery, and shoemaker's shop, and had acquired the responsibilities of a major citizen of Furnace Village. Despite his new encumbrances, however, he had nothing but respect and admiration for John Chipman. John had done what Gamaliel had long had on his con-

12

science to do before Elisha sold his holdings. Momentarily he was torn between the call of pioneering in the Grants and developing his assorted interests in Furnace Village. For years John and Gamaliel had been fast friends, though they had little in common. John was as rambunctious as Elisha, but along with his impetuosity and daring he had enough tact and refinement to appeal to Gamaliel's cautious conservatism. They were a good team, and to certify their fondness for each other, Gamaliel decided to marry John's sister Abigail. She had the Chipman determination and fluency of speech, the solidity of character and physique, and the Chipman disregard of the fastidious. She could handle a hoe and a musket with the same facility that she could handle a ladle or a good argument. She was not beautiful, she was not gracious, but a suitor as ungainly as Gamaliel could hardly expect to win the belle of Salisbury. She had learned from her brother as much as anyone knew about the Champlain Valley and decided it would make the ideal home site for her and the husband of her choice, but with their marriage late in August of 1767, plans for taking up residence in the New Hampshire Grants were once more put aside. Painter was not one to permit the exposure of his bride to the vicissitudes of an unknown land.

In fact, Gamaliel would probably have been content to spend the rest of his life in Salisbury, living a sober and undistinguished existence in a well regulated household, if it had not been for the constant reminders of Abigail that the real opportunities were farther north. In his middle twenties he was neither prepossessing in appearance nor commanding in address. He was a steady, practical farmer and handy-man. Only his sharp eye and determined jaw seemed to contradict the sluggish conservatism. His moderate height and natural shyness rarely made him a center of attention, though once given responsibility and the opportunity to demonstrate his slow wisdom, his neighbors could suspect that he had potentialities as a leader. But what he accomplished, he accomplished by deliberation and determination rather than through graciousness of appeal or glow of wit.

Family life called for greater refinement than his rude bachelor household offered, and before Christmas in 1768 he sold his farm and moved to the spacious Chipman family home which had been sorely in need of the attentions of a man since the death of Abigail's father. His first son Joseph was born in October 1770, and Painter settled into quiet domesticity on the Chipman farm, and spent less time with the rowdy veterans of Canadian wars. When Samuel was born two years later, pioneering in Champlain Valley appeared even more remote, despite the polemics of Abigail. But late in the autumn of 1772 John Chipman made up his mind; he allied himself with one of the principal Salisbury mechanics, Abisha Washburn, married his daughter Sarah, and decided to take his new bride to Middlebury. Abisha intended to put up a sawmill in Middlebury with John's assistance. Would Gamaliel join them? Deliverance Spaulding wanted to sell the lot next to John's clearing, and Gamaliel could get it for little more than the asking. Gamaliel weighed the prospects, and they were anything but promising. He considered the feasibility of taking two infants into a wilderness, and saw the impossibilities. But the arguments of Abigail, John and Sarah were convincing and conclusive. They had a way of converting the impossible into a challenge. And at last Gamaliel's long-implanted family weakness to be on the move cropped out. Casting aside his caution he ceremoniously purchased the two-hundred acre lot next to John's, and the

14

two families spent the winter laying plans for a long expedition.

1773 was a critical year in New England history. The three-pence Tea Tax was converting smugglers into patriots in Philadelphia, New York and Boston. The British revenue cutter *Gaspee* was treacherously scuttled by Rhode Island rioters in Narragansett Bay. Great Britain was facing the decision as to whether or not she possessed any authority over the "haughty American Republicans," and George III was concluding that "we must master them or totally leave them to themselves and treat them as aliens." Litchfield County in northwestern Connecticut was too far off the route of political traffic to be appreciably affected by squabbles between seacoast towns and the mother country. The squabbles made good tavern talk, but few took them seriously. It never occurred to Painter or John Chipman that in moving two hundred miles further inland from the Atlantic they could be moving to a rebellious frontier, though according to alarmist reports brought back from Bennington by their fellow townsman, Ethan Allen, it might be necessary to be on guard against the covetous Yorkers who had designs on some of the New Hampshire towns. Gamaliel had no intention of being a patriot or becoming one. He had no ideological cause to fight for, no higher purpose than the reluctant urge to build a home in a new country, to gain the satisfaction of winning a struggle against the forest, the elements, and whoever dared resist his efforts. During the winter the sorting of all the personal possessions—the few that were to be taken and the many that were to be left behind—was more like the preparation for an internment than for a long-anticipated journey.

It was a journey from which there could be no turning back.

15

The grim realization of it came to them poignantly in the little ceremony at the Town Hall where the names of John Chipman, Gamaliel Painter, and Abigail Painter were affixed to the deed of the home farm, certifying that they "for the Consideration of Two Hundred twenty Pounds fourteen shillings two Pence halfpenny Lawful Money received to our full Satisfaction Do therefore give grant bargain Sell & confirm unto the s⁴ Nath¹ Buell his Heirs and Assigns forever Eighty four Acres and one Hundred forty & two rods of Land in s⁴ Salisbury being part of the Farm that John Chipman late of s⁴ Salisbury deceast lived on . . ."

And the last tie was broken on April 13 when they signed a quitclaim releasing "all the Right and Title that we have Ever had or ought to have in and unto all that Part of the farm of land in Salisbury that belonged to our Honoured Father John Chipman Late of Said Salisbury Deceast that was Distributed or Set off to our Honoured Mother . . ." Neither the Chipmans nor the Painters had a home in Salisbury to which they could return if the venture should go badly.

The shadbush was still white on the Berkshire hillside as the two families plodded precariously north in the Spring of 1773 with their two-wheeled ox cart piled high with tools, plump meal sacks, kettles, and babies. Gamaliel drove the oxen, Abigail followed on horseback. Acres of trillium blanketed the rough slopes; the marshes were gilded with cowslips, and countless shades of green spread the landscape of any open vista. The woods, the mountains, and the scent of spring let them forget the pain of departure.

Through the hills the road wound north to Canaan, crossed the line to the Colony of Massachusetts and led to Sheffield,

Great Barrington, Lenox, Pittsfield and Williamstown, then into New Hampshire and through Pownal, Bennington, Manchester, Rutland and Pittsford. There were days when they could travel as much as thirty miles, and others when ten was a laborious journey because of the mountains and the mud. Through Massachusetts the road was well cut and well rutted, and other travellers occasionally joined the slow, tired procession. Taverns offered overnight refuge at settlements like Stockbridge and Pittsfield, but they were not loath to camp in the open or take advantage of the yard, ham and broad hearth of an isolated settler. Once in New Hampshire the going was harder and hospitality undependable. The longest stretch, between Manchester and Rutland, was the most desolate, and the occupants of the few log cabins they passed appeared to have escaped by design to a place where they could never be found. Yet they were going still further north. At Rutland, nearing their destination, they met the semblance of a military highway that had been built across the mountains from Charlestown to Crown Point over a decade before. It was in hopeless disrepair, soon turned west, and the party were on their own to follow as best they could the blazed trail along the Otter Creek. Seven years before when John Chipman and his fifteen companions had reached Pittsford, they despaired of the slow progress with their ox cart, and instead of cutting their way through the forest had built a log raft, managed to mount the cart on it and float it down the Creek, but with only two men it was easier now to cut the way through. Late on a May afternoon with the sun throwing long yellow shadows across the valley, the Painters and Chipmans drove into the overgrown clearing that John had once hopefully begun, and halted the oxen in front of a weathered lean-to. The Painters and Chipmans were home.

Gamaliel Painter was canny enough to be fully aware before he left Connecticut that the title to his land at Middlebury was as clear as Indian pudding. New Hampshire claimed that its own border extended as far west as did the boundaries of Connecticut and Massachusetts, twenty miles from the Hudson. New York had been granted everything as far east as the Connecticut River. Both claims included Champlain Valley. France had been forced to yield its protectorate over the Valley only ten years before, and "Sieur Hocquort" who owned this particular seigniory of New France had sold it to one Michael Chartier Lotbiniere in 1763 when France surrendered Canada to the British. Lotbiniere in absentia was still perseveringly prosecuting his claim to what a group of squatters from Connecticut insisted on labeling Middlebury. Previously Godfrey Dellius had bought the same tract from the Mohawks and had the sale confirmed under the New York seal, and Colonel John Henry Lydius had also unwittingly purchased from the Mohawks most of the lower Champlain Valley and had his title confirmed by the Governor of the Province of Massachusetts Bay. He in turn divided it into townships and sold them to several hundred British subjects in Connecticut.

Painter had a business eye and a legal sense. He knew all about the uncertainty of his title, or knew enough to realize that titles to the towns on either flank of the Green Mountains were the subject of delicate dispute. His peripatetic friend Ethan Allen, commuting between Salisbury and points north, would have told him if no one else had. He disregarded it more candidly than did a majority of the hesitant grant

18

holders. Yankee philosophy decreed two truths: occupation was nine tenths of the law, and right of defense went with anything properly paid for and taken possession of. Gamaliel had seen the charter, signed and sealed by Benning Wentworth. Indirectly he had paid for his share of the twenty pounds which was the purchase price of Middlebury. He had only to occupy the two hundred acres and establish signs of residence. The power of Great Britain should be behind his grant, Governor Wentworth should defend it, and incidentally the Church of England, for the Governor had, with more political perspicacity than religious zeal, given the Church a pitch in each of the towns.

Once a house looked lived in and the land looked worked, a settler had much more secure tenure, so Painter's principal objective the first year was to establish himself, plant his roots deep and let a lot of sunlight into the Valley. Sunlight was of first importance. No one was anybody but a squatter until he had made a huge gap in the forest. During the spring and summer the pillar of fire by night and the cloud of smoke by day rarely left the Valley. The air was thick with choking fumes from smouldering green trees, tops and brush, as acre after acre of virgin forest was leveled by Painter and Chipman, with a good deal of help from their wives.

Communal housekeeping was first set up in the lean-to on the plot John had cleared seven years before. The clearing had reverted to a tangle of brush and saplings, but with scythe and axe it was a small task to cut and burn the new growth in comparison with the labor of felling timber. As the young sumac, thistles, birch and evergreen disappeared, the gloom of the forest was transformed into a sunlit area. The shadows shortened and the mountains thrust up to the east. A garden patch was dug next to the lean-to and left for Abigail and Sarah to plant while baby-tending and housekeeping. The two woodsmen set off for Gamaliel's adjacent pitch.

John had given Gamaliel good advice when he urged him to purchase Spaulding's lot. It was far superior to the land he would have owned if he had kept Elisha's plot. If anything, John had underestimated its value. The site had served for centuries as a camp ground for transient Indian tribes. It was already partially cleared, the surface was fine alluvial soil, and it was well stocked with useful tools and utensils which the Iroquois had buried or abandoned: stone hammers, gouges and chisels, arrowheads, pots and pestles. To be sure, there was no certainty that brown-skinned warriors would not show up again with the expectation of using the camp in transit to another rendezvous of pillage, but Painter calculated that the advantages were greater than the potential dangers.

His two hundred acres were carefully marked off that year with "buts and bounds as follows: beginning on his north line . . . at a heap of stones on the ledge by the river, thence east thirty-seven degrees south fifty-six rods to a stake, then south thirty-seven degrees west one hundred and sixty rods to a red ash tree, thence west thirty-seven degrees north two hundred rods to a large maple, then north thirty-seven degrees east one hundred and sixty rods to a hard maple, then to the first mentioned bounds . . ."

Everything called to be done at once. The most urgent need was a substantial shelter for Abigail and the children. While the fires of forest destruction were kept crackling, every available hour of daylight during May and early June was spent in cutting, hauling and notching logs for their cabin. The straightest, the soundest, and the nearest pines were taken,

20

without reference to the king's command "that all white and other pine trees, fit for masting our Royal Navy be carefully preserved for that purpose." The four walls, solid as a fort, homely and crude, rose rapidly. Allowance for doors and windows was disregarded. They could readily be cut out later. Abigail and Sarah, as time from their household duties permitted, were set to work stripping heaps of elm bark with which to shingle the roof.

Food not only for the summer but also for the winter was an ever-present concern. There were always plenty of pike in the Creek, but fish was a poor meat substitute for men and women working sixteen hours a day. Hours had to be wasted tracking down venison or bear, hauling in the catch, dressing and hanging the quarters. And the oxen were put to work on the slow job of plowing a cornfield, weaving in and out among the stubborn stumps. Roots had to be chopped out, boulders hauled aside, sod loosened and turned.

Before the end of July the winter crop of turnips was in, the corn was knee high, the parsnips were showing strong tops, and the squash were sending out runners toward the forest. The two families had moved into the unfinished log shelter, and the floor of loose bark was well-packed. Cooking was still done in the yard, and the gaping hole cut for the fireplace and chimney was unfilled. There was plenty of time to complete them before frost. Gamaliel was well aware that the first year defeated most settlers who were going to be defeated, but thanks to the two-family effort, better progress was being made than they had counted on. If there were no setbacks, if the weather held good, and the deer could be kept out of the corn, they could conquer the first season.

As the summer advanced, a half dozen other parties arrived

21

to put in a few weeks of work on their pitches. Benjamin Smalley, the first to complete his cabin, had the whole Middlebury population in for a housewarming. Eleazar Slasson and Jim Owen commenced clearings to the south and started work on a cabin for Slasson. Near by, Sam Bentley was building a log barn and Joshua Hyde was puttering away at a small clearing. The arrival of every newcomer was an occasion for celebration, joshing, and swapping of Connecticut gossip. Others on their way to Weybridge, New Haven or Vergennes, occasionally made detours to the Painters to bring news of latest developments in the colonies. Affairs were not going well with Great Britain; New York authorities were officially grumbling about the trespass of settlers on land east of Lake Champlain and were parcelling out to their subjects the same land which had already been sold by Governor Wentworth; New Hampshire had stopped talking back. There was the possibility that the one hundred and thirty towns between the Connecticut and Lake Champlain to which Benning Wentworth had granted charters might be left on their own, for the king had again decreed that the Connecticut River was the rightful boundary between New York and New Hampshire. Petitions and insistent appeals for a reversal of the decision were on their way across the Atlantic, but for the time being New Hampshire could take no drastic action nor raise any objection if occupants of the Grants changed their allegiance to New York. Many were doing it. In any case the controversy with New York was now automatically transferred from the New Hampshire governor to the claimants, and rather than pay for their charters a second time, the more courageous among the grant owners were taking the law into their own hands. "Committees of Safety" were being elected to serve their own judicial purposes, and volunteer militia, dubbed the Green Mountain Boys, were more active in enforcing the collective will.

By fall, Gamaliel for the first time was seriously concerned about the authenticity of his title. The few months in the Valley had convinced him that Middlebury had a future. He wanted to stay. But with his own sweat and worry being expended on a pitch, it was well to have assurance that the property would not suddenly become someone's else, particularly at the passing whim of an Albany or London politician intent on bestowing a feudal estate on some gentry. Gamaliel could quickly settle his right of ownership by making a trip to Albany and paying five shillings sterling in quitrent for his two hundred acres. He could afford it and promptly become a bona fide citizen of New York. But he was enough of an insurgent to recognize the injustice of paying such a fee. When he came to the Grants he came with his gun, anticipating that he might have to use it.

2 REBEL

Gamaliel Painter was introduced to the kind of guerrilla warfare that went on in the New Hampshire Grants prior to the Revolution, on the afternoon of the tenth of August 1773, when a posse of a hundred Green Mountain Boys, headed by Ethan Allen, halted their horses in the yard of his frontier cabin at the south end of Middlebury. It was not the same Ethan Allen that Gamaliel had known in Salisbury, Connecticut. Now he carried the label of Colonel Commandant and was ludicrously arrayed in a flashy uniform decorated with more crimson piping than modesty demanded. Gamaliel's caution and Ethan's abandon had never led to any consuming friendship; they had accepted each other for what they were.

25

The greetings were hearty and friendly enough, but Ethan made it quite clear that his subordinate was addressing an officer. Gamaliel never forgot it.

There was business to be done and the Colonel Commandant came to the point. The boys were on their way to Panton, twenty miles northwest, to oust the trespassing Yorker John Reid from his claim. Reid had been raided a year before, and after the incident Allen had addressed an extravagant letter of double talk to the Governor of New York: "We do humbly assure your excellency we have no disposition of alienation of affection . . . Nevertheless such locations and settlements on our lands would be incompatible with friendship . . ." Despite the warning, Reid had brazenly returned with a following of Scotch immigrants to rebuild a village on the falls of Otter Creek. Governor Tryon apparently had the effrontery to defy Ethan Allen in allowing Colonel Reid to return to Panton. Would Gamaliel join the Boys in their attempt to measure out justice?

Painter and Chipman left the oxen for Abigail to stable, shouldered axes and flintlocks, and joined the raiders. That afternoon Gamaliel became a soldier. At heart he was not a soldier. He was a pacifist given to cool deliberation, a man much more appropriately seated on a judgment stool than on a war saddle, but he was caught up in a frontier society that called for soldiering. He became a soldier through devotion to that society and through the circumstances it had created.

What followed at Panton the next day was shocking to his sensibilities, repulsive to his very being. It was clumsy, cowardly, barbaric. Bordering the Creek was the start of a neat village, a row of cabins nearing completion, a grist mill in

26

operation at the falls, acres of ripening corn, grain and vege-
tables—the sort of scene he was straining every muscle day
after weary day to complete. What would take him years to
do, they had already done.

The small army crept to the edge of the clearing, dispersed
and half surrounded it. At a signal they turned desperados
and rushed like yelping Indians into the settlement. Helpless
Scotch artisans climbed down from their scaffolding in time
to see the flames licking up the walls from the dry debris
scattered beneath. Men stood terrified in the fields watching
haystacks turn into pyramids of flame. The miller cowered
in a corner while the priceless grindstones were wrenched out,
broken and heaved over the falls. The mill was burned. Cattle
were turned into the cornfield, and marauders charged in on
their horses to trample down what could not otherwise be
destroyed.

It was wanton, scorched-earth destruction in a land that
needed every kernel of grain and every hour of labor. And the
Green Mountain Boys made a sport of it. They lined up the
terrified Scotsmen and threatened to skin them alive if their
exodus was not complete and immediate. Looking at the
ruins, the Scotsmen had every reason to believe that the
threats would be carried out. The destruction was over in an
hour, but before the invaders departed they made sure that
the Scotch settlers were well on their way back toward New
York.

To Gamaliel Painter, sober, deliberate and mild-mannered,
seldom given to intense action, the attack was the height of
savagery. It was his initiation as a member of the Green
Mountain Boys, and regardless of his preference for quieter
forms of recreation, from now on until there was no longer

any doubt about who were the masters of the valleys east and west of the Green Mountains, he could expect to make such excursions with increasing regularity. He could expect at any moment of the day to be called upon to drop his spade, his scythe, his adze, and follow an excited informant to a rendezvous of the pillagers. There could no longer be any assurance of tranquil nights on the edge of the Otter.

He was a sworn member of the fraternity of vandals and defenders of democratic faith, the Green Mountain Boys. He was a knight errant pledged to the purpose of keeping the Grants out of the hands of despotic Yorkers. It was his duty individually to spy out any intruder from New York or any recalcitrant settler who dared express doubt as to who held the authority in Champlain Valley. His intelligence was reported to what was generally agreed upon as Headquarters, Fay's Tavern in Bennington. Upon a signal or a passed word, the mounties would assemble and descend upon the culprit twenty strong, fifty, or a hundred, depending on the nature of the offense and the strength of the offenders. He wore a sprig of spruce in his cap as a symbol of his membership, adopted the secret war cry *Cuck-a-ca-do-ca-doo* and solemnly agreed to affix the great seal of the company with discrimination and alacrity, the mark to be applied with a beech withe on the naked back of an offender in confirmation of the great red seal of New Hampshire. Banishment followed the application. It was a raucous, disrespectful, frequently intoxicated clan, ready, as occasion demanded, to fire a home, afflict brutal chastisement, defy the stoutest authority, or tenderly reinstate a family which had suffered injustice in the hands of the enemy. Arguments were settled conclusively out of a courtroom. They were the military force and the judicial body

28

serving an informal committee of town representatives which forbade all inhabitants in the District of the New Hampshire Grants to take "grants or confirmation of grants under the government of New York," or "to hold, take or accept any office of honor or profit under the Colony of New York."

In turn Gamaliel Painter was among those accused by the General Assembly of New York of "many acts of outrage, cruelty and oppression . . . perpetrated by a number of lawless persons . . . who have seized, insulted and terrified several magistrates and other civil officers . . . , assumed to themselves military commands and judicial power, burned and demolished the houses and property, and beat and abused the persons of many of his Majesty's subjects." Painter took with a grain of salt the angry warning that "if any person or persons, either secretly or openly, shall, unlawfully, wilfully and maliciously burn or destroy the grain, corn, or hay of any other person . . . , demolish or pull down any dwelling house, barn, stable, gristmill, saw-mill, or out-house, . . . the offenders therein shall be adjudged felons, and shall suffer death . . ."

Instead of promoting terror and a new allegiance, the empty threats were accepted with contempt; instead of breaking resistance, they alerted an offensive. The Green Mountain Boys could readily match any force of constabulary dispatched to the Grants to enforce the bold warning. For two years the verbal broadsides were exchanged while Yorkers continued to receive humiliation, banishment, torture and a generous number of stripes for their loyalties, while the settlement of Middlebury slowly took on life and cultivation. Summer twice faded into brilliant autumn, and autumn into gray November. Squash and pumpkin were heaped in corners of the

Painter cabin; a few bushels of nubbin corn were stored on the loft to dry; the parsnips, beets and turnips were buried in a dug-out. The winters were long and slow with rarely a word from outside the snow-burdened valley. The wolves howled boldly and persistently in the crisp sub-zero nights. The food was monotonous, the company was monotonous, the labor was monotonous, the weather was monotonous. Inside the log hut the family of four lived in a perpetual chill and in perpetual twilight, with the only illumination coming from the fireplace and the cloth-covered windows, and the only entertainment from the two moppets, Samuel and Joseph, who took more pleasure than their parents in the meal preparation, in the wildcat whining from a nearby tree, in the dull snowy evenings, the tool sharpening and the pelt scraping.

Most of the other settlers went back to Connecticut for the winter. They returned in the Spring of 1774 with news that the Port of Boston had been closed, the Massachusetts Bay Charter annulled, that a new law had been issued requiring that manslaughter cases involving British servants in America were in the future to be tried in British courts, that the Grant towns as well as the villages of southern New England could expect the responsibility of quartering British troops. In the Spring of 1775 they returned with the appalling news of Lexington and Concord.

Painter had listened to a lot of loose talk from radicals about separation and independence, but fighting rebellion against his mother country had never seriously crossed his mind. He was a conservative and loyal colonial of Great Britain, ready to insist on receiving all the rights, privileges and benefits that went with his allegiance. His stake in the

Grants even now depended on a decision from London. But in less than a month after Lexington, he had to revise all his ideas on pacifism.

It was on the march to Lexington that Benedict Arnold, brooding on the desperate need for artillery in Boston, conceived the idea of plundering the old French fort at Ticonderoga and hauling the cannon to the defense of Massachusetts. He knew that there was a magnificent arsenal on Lake Champlain, an arsenal that would take months to duplicate in New England foundries, and he knew that it was being protected by a garrison of not more than two or three score redcoats. Fort Ticonderoga had to be taken despite what its capture might do to the cause of appeasement.

On April 30, when his name was still on the tongue of every Middlesex County patriot, and greater battles than Lexington appeared imminent, he addressed a letter to the Massachusetts Committee of Safety informing them that "there are at Ticonderoga eighty pieces of heavy cannon, twenty brass guns, from four to eighteen pounders, and ten to twelve large mortars." The Committee was impressed. Within three days he held a commission as Colonel and orders to "proceed with all expedition . . . to the Fort at Ticonderoga, and use your best endeavors to reduce the same, taking possession of the cannon, mortars, stores, &c." He was to enlist four hundred men, and after capturing the Fort, bring back the cannon to Cambridge, "leaving behind what may be necessary to secure that post, with a sufficient garrison."

Benedict Arnold was carrying rebellion and violence into Gamaliel Painter's backyard. Late in the afternoon of the ninth of May, Sam Beach, a Whiting blacksmith with whom Gamaliel had served on the Valley raids and scouting trips,

31

strode into the Painter clearing and in the name of the Green Mountain Boys presented verbal orders to report at once to Hands Cove at Shoreham with arms and ample ammunition. The perspiring Beach could spare little time for conversation; he was on a sixty-mile circuit of Champlain Valley and had to complete his mission within twenty-four hours. Over the fortified jug he explained that Colonel Arnold had sent the alert to the Green Mountain Boys and urged them to be ready to join several hundred other recruits that would be marching north for an assault on Ticonderoga. The Boys had received the condescending request, held a council of war and decided they could do without the assistance of foreigners from Massachusetts and Connecticut in carrying out a minor operation like capturing a Fort.

Ticonderoga, less than twenty miles from Middlebury, was vital to Painter's interests, as well as to the interests of Great Britain. This northern Gibraltar of the Colonies was a major Fort in the long life line extending from Montreal down the Richelieu, through Lake Champlain and Lake George to the Hudson and New York. Possession of it could determine not only Painter's immediate future but also the future of the Colonies, its loss would be a stark humiliation to the British, and he fully realized what the consequences would be in attempted reprisals on the Green Mountain settlements.

Painter the pacifist and Painter the opportunist had to make quick reconciliation; but circumstance again had predetermined his course. Beach explained that headquarters had been set up at Remington's Tavern in Castleton with Ethan Allen in command of the expeditionary forces, that close to one hundred and fifty had already reported in, and that thirty of them had been despatched to Skenesborough at the southern end of Champlain to capture boats for ferrying the troops from Hands Cove to the Fort. Allen would proceed that evening to Shoreham, and Painter could meet the company there. Gamaliel had been nominated as a rebel against Great Britain. He accepted the nomination. Before sunset he headed west with John Chipman and a following of other volunteers from the vicinity of Middlebury.

The Colonel Commandant and most of the delegation from Castleton had arrived at the Cove before them, but the boats expected from Skenesborough were nowhere in sight. As the motley party of Grant settlers and Connecticut farmers waited that night hour after hour on the chill shore of the Lake, Painter began to question more and more the wisdom of their venture. Should the Green Mountain Boys take upon themselves the responsibility for precipitating a break with Great Britain? A skirmish of this sort was typical of the rash action into which Allen had repeatedly led them. It was the recklessness and irresponsibility of Ethan Allen that most disturbed Painter now, his swaggering, his blasphemy, his vulgarity. He was not the kind of leader such a grim enterprise called for.

Above the subdued murmur of the impatient company, Allen kept up his constant flow of rhetoric, railing against the Almighty for the delay, as if profanity could make their transportation materialize. Still the boats did not arrive. The whole expedition was in danger of failure, for dawn would put an end to their plans within two hours. It was two o'clock. Suddenly a hush fell over the confused crowd. Even Allen's cursing was momentarily muted. A lane was made through the throng as a sentry led a strange officer through to the Colonel Commandant. He was mounted on a magnificent horse, was impressively and handsomely uniformed, plumes waving from his hat, gold epaulets and stripes glimmering out of the darkness. The effect would not have been different if the angel Gabriel to whom Allen had been making frequent references, had appeared instead of Colonel Benedict Arnold.

But when Arnold opened up with a verbal lashing of Allen for not biding his time and announced that from that moment he was taking command of the expedition, the undisciplined Green Mountaineers responded with a unified snarl that would have given pause to any seasoned officer, and Allen out-bellowed them all with new fulmination, the eloquence of which Painter had never heard before. Arnold produced orders from the Massachusetts Committee of Safety. Allen matched them with orders from his own Committee of War. Both were authentic, and neither officer was ready to acknowledge that one could supersede the other. Arnold was too proud to give a point; Allen too pompous. Secretly Painter wished that the Colonel Commandant might be put in his place for once. Painter was ready to admire any officer that held his ground with Ethan Allen. If Arnold could be made to shed all the finery, he could make a mighty good leader. But no one dared give voice to Gamaliel's treacherous thoughts. The majority overwhelmingly supported the leader they had duly elected, and refused to have anything to do with an expedition commanded by the usurper. The capture of Ticonderoga had become a minor issue compared to the issue over precedence, when abruptly they were summoned to their senses by the call from a sentry that a ship had been sighted. All eyes turned toward the Lake. A great scow, hugging the gray shoreline was slowly moving toward the beach. Arguments were forgotten as it plowed in. The scow, bor-

34

rowed from a neighbor on the Lake, had miraculously broken the stalemate, and Allen with becoming charity quietly gave Arnold permission to go aboard and share the command.

Gamaliel was close behind Allen and Arnold when they stormed past the dazed sentry at Fort Ticonderoga just before dawn that morning. There had been room in the scow for only eighty-three, and the assault was made by them before there was time to ferry others to the New York shore. It was all over in ten minutes. Side by side the Colonel and the Colonel Commandant crashed the gate and took possession. Fort Ticonderoga nominally belonged to the Continental Congress. But if the daring of Ethan Allen made any impression on Painter, the cool defiance of Benedict Arnold made a greater one. Arnold had demonstrated that he was equal to any of the machinations of the Green Mountain Boys. Painter admired him.

By sunrise the easy victory had turned into an extravagant celebration: Ticonderoga was magnificently stocked with liquor as well as war gear and, to Arnold's horror, the victors were far more interested in repairing their own spirits than in repairing the crumbling Fort. Against the co-commander's protests, the Boys proceeded to empty the precious British casks, and under the influence, the celebration quickly turned into a party of rapacious plundering. "The power is now taken out of my hands," wrote Arnold to his Committee of Safety, as soon as he realized that affairs were completely out of hand. "I am not consulted, nor have I a voice in any matters. There is here at present near one hundred men who are in the greatest confusion and anarchy, destroying and plundering private property, committing every enormity, and paying no attention to public service. . . . Everything is governed by whim and caprice; the soldiers threatening to leave the garrison on the least affront. . . . As I have, in consequence of my orders from you, gentlemen, been the first person who entered and took possession of the Fort, I shall keep it, at every hazard, until I have further advice and orders. . . ."

Allen was sober enough to know that he would be held to account for his conduct and the conduct of his forces, and hurriedly dashed off one version of the conquest directly to the Massachusetts Congress and another to the Albany Committee. The Provincial Congress of Massachusetts, sitting at Watertown, was informed that he had taken the Fortress of Ticonderoga by storm, as ordered by the General Assembly of the Colony of Connecticut, that "the soldiery behaved with uncommon rancour when they leaped into the Fort," and that Colonel Arnold had "greatly contributed to the taking of the Fortress." To the New York Committee Allen more generously conceded that "Colonel Arnold entered the fortress with me side by side."

Everyone at the Fort with any semblance of authority or official responsibility also took to letter writing by way of defending what had transpired. But to those within the Fort the animosity and confusion was far more evident than it could ever be to the recipients of the contradictory letters. Painter saw the confusion first-hand and was shocked. He was not one to ignore opportunities for imbibing free rum within the limits of moderation, but he could not tolerate disorder for an occasion that demanded decorum and discipline. In the two days following the capture of the Fort he lost most of the limited respect he had ever had for Ethan Allen. By comparison Colonel Arnold was a dignified and noble com-

36

mander. Painter unhesitatingly let Arnold know where his sympathies lay. Arnold remembered it.

When Crown Point, eight miles to the north, was surrendered with its modest garrison, there was further cause for celebrating, and when the captured British schooner at last put in from Skenesborough, the last of the King's grog kegs were emptied in toasts to the captors and their cause. The ship had arrived too late to do any ferrying of troops, but it was promptly rechristened *Liberty*, and Colonel Arnold, seeing possible relief from his embarrassment as quasi-commander of the Fort, took command of the ship and announced his intention of using it for a raid on St. Johns, a hundred miles north on the Richelieu River. The Boys raised no objection; the strategy was sound, but they were loath to sail on the same craft, and run the risk of appearing to cooperate with Arnold. Regretting that they had not thought of the venture first, they determined on an independent operation and took off in flat-bottomed bateaux rigged with square blanket sails and oars on a race up the Lake against the *Liberty*.

For a week Gamaliel Painter did more steady rowing than he was called upon to do the rest of his life. Arnold won the race with his contingent of thirty-five men, took St. Johns, its garrison of a sergeant and twelve men, His Majesty's sloop with her crew of seven, burned several bateaux and departed in the captured sloop. On the way back they encountered Allen's ninety starving oarsmen still tugging at the sweeps, generously contributed enough provisions to revive them, and tried to persuade them to give up their "wild, impractical scheme," but Ethan Allen was not to be persuaded. Once the Green Mountain Boys had set their sights on a destination, they were not easily reversed. They had to take St. Johns too.

37

They continued north, captured the town, and confidently bedded down for the night on the beach. The lake air, the long pull and perhaps the celebration potions proved conducive to sound sleep. If a watch was set, he was too exhausted to keep it. In any case the Boys were awakened the next morning by a shower of grapeshot from the opposite shore, and so little time was wasted in making a retreat that three of the men were left behind still in deep slumber.

By May 21 when the last bateau pulled in at Crown Point, Gamaliel and the other farm boys from across the Lake had experienced a long enough escapade to last them at least until the crops were in. They left Colonel Commandant Allen and Colonel Arnold squabbling over whose rank took precedence at the Forts and deferentially took leave with the warning from Ethan ringing in their ears that they would soon be routed out to capture Montreal. They could be spared temporarily, for reinforcements had arrived from southern New England, and among them Gamaliel's brother Elisha, with enough determination and egotism to make up for Gamaliel's lack of enthusiasm for soldiering.

Back in Middlebury there was small satisfaction in planting corn that might be harvested by Britishers or their Indian allies. But against the faint hope that Ticonderoga might be held, Gamaliel put in his seed with the help of Abigail, Joseph and young Samuel. Late in June the report of the Battle of Bunker Hill came in, and a quite irrelevant report that Ethan Allen and Seth Warner had tired of writing letters and had gone personally to Philadelphia to urge that the Green Mountain Boys be formed into a military regiment with officers of their own choosing and recognized by the New York command. Ethan usually got what he demanded, and

Gamaliel could well make up his mind that he would soon be on the march again. There were calls for surveying jobs and he tempered his suspense tramping the swamps, ledges and thickets of Otter Valley with his chains and sextant.

The Continental Congress and the New York Assembly meantime approved the request for the Green Mountain regiment, and late in July at Kent's Tavern in Dorset, Gamaliel had the satisfaction of helping to elect Seth Warner as his Colonel Commandant in place of Allen by a vote of forty-one to five. Gamaliel, like most of his more moderate associates, had seen enough of Ethan's impetuous action, his over-confidence, his rum, and his recklessness. Before leaving Dorset the representatives were assured that they would soon have a handsome green uniform with red facing to wear on an invasion of Canada.

During the middle of September, Gamaliel was completing a survey of two lots for Samuel Moulton in Cornwall, so he did not join Warner's hundred and seventy Green Mountain Rangers who reported at St. Johns on the sixteenth. But when he showed up a few days later with a detachment of some seventy late-comers, he found an entirely different St. Johns from the town he had hastily deserted on the unlucky morning in May. Now it was heavily fortified and General Montgomery was laying seige to it with hundreds of entrenched men. The Rangers, however, were detailed north on a scouting maneuver, and then on to Longueuil across the river from Montreal. They were not attached to the heterogeneous group of a hundred and ten Canadian recruits with which Ethan Allen, without benefit of commission, attempted to capture Montreal in a prima donna assault. At Longueuil, Painter learned of the fiasco and Allen's capture, appreciating the

39

censure of General Washington: "Colonel Allen's misfortune will, I hope, teach a lesson of prudence and subordination to others who may be too ambitious to outshine their general officers and . . . rush into enterprises which . . . are destructive to themselves." His impetuous boyhood friend was now on his way to England in chains.

The assignment at Longueuil was monotonous, cold and uneventful except for an occasional skirmish with scouts from across the St. Lawrence. The crude encampment overlooked a ten-mile stretch of the river which any force bound for St. Johns would have to cross. It was not until the last day of October that Painter experienced his first Canadian fighting. Boats were sighted making the dash to the opposite shore. The armada increased to thirty-four craft filled with Canadians, regulars and Indians bound for St. Johns to relieve the beleaguered forces there. Not one of the enemy ever reached the Longueuil side unscathed. The attack was smashed in midstream with a loss to the British of fifty men, and not a casualty among the Rangers. St. Johns surrendered a few days later. The shivering, sick American army then advanced to take Montreal and Quebec, but Painter and the Rangers did not accompany it. Their enlistment period was running out; they disagreed with Montgomery, refused to believe that he had the strength and equipment to succeed. They received their discharge and through the autumn snow tramped away from disaster, back to the indifferent shelters of rugged comfort in the Grants, though Elisha remained in Canada, to establish his reputation as a soldier and to complain about "the cold, the wet, the mud, and the mire."

The winter quiet in the settlement belied the true state of affairs beyond the horizon to the north. Painter and his fellow

Rangers were not permitted to enjoy civilian status for long. On the last day of the year, Montgomery's depleted and frosted army met with even greater calamity than the Rangers had foreseen, and an urgent call was sent to Warner pleading with him to come to the rescue. Painter agreed to re-enlist, but first he had to fulfill his legislative duties at Deacon Fay's tavern where the town representatives were called on January 16, 1776 to expend more elocutionary energy on grievances against New York and to beg the Continental Congress not to place the Grants under New York either for geographical or military delineation: "We, your honours' humble petitioners, most earnestly pray your honours to take our case into your wise consideration, and order that for the future your petitioners shall do duty in the continental service, if required, as inhabitants of said New Hampshire grants." What Allen and Warner had accomplished for them the previous summer they now wished to retract. Gamaliel's affirmative vote made approval of the petition unanimous; in fact he may well have had a hand in whittling out the sententious document.

In late February Painter plodded north on snowshoes along with the ill-clad, ill-equipped army of over four hundred Rangers, arriving at the pestilence-ridden encampment in Canada on March fifth. But it was an utterly futile march. Less than a third of the three thousand already there were fit for duty and four hundred could scarcely compensate for those incapacitated by smallpox, frostbite, and the pall of defeat. They were without clothes, beds, blankets, medicine or discipline.

But it was the long hopeless period of waiting, scouting and occasional collision with the enemy that changed Painter's career for the rest of the war. At the Chambly encampment, ten miles west of Montreal, Painter first had the opportunity to meet Colonel Jeduthan Baldwin, who had been ordered to Canada by Washington to plan counter fortifications for Quebec. Colonel Baldwin was an uncommonly gifted, though unlettered, engineer, an unsung hero of the Battle of Bunker Hill, who modestly confessed that he went there "by an invitation . . . and threw up a breastwork and was on that hill the whole of that memorable day." Many of the major fortifications around Boston and New York were the product of his genius, and among his military engagements he had sandwiched enough social engagements with General and Mrs. George Washington to establish himself with most of the Revolutionary gold braid.

Colonel Baldwin was an indispensable man in the New York theatre of operations, but the northern terminus of the lifeline between Manhattan and Quebec was even more vital at the moment, so the indispensable Baldwin was sent to the more important post in Canada, and at Chambly he found an able lieutenant in Gamaliel Painter. Together they suffered the same privations, distemper, tedium, suspense. "We have a Very Gloomy account of our army at Quebeck," scribbled the Colonel. "The report is that bout 500 of our men (chiefly sick) are taken prisoners with the artillery & stores, but no Sertainty . . . a great Battle fought but noboddy Killd & noboddy Hurt . . ." The epidemic struck, but it could not strike down their pride: "the pox this Day began to fill . . . Stomach Very Soar & Squamish loathing every Kind of food . . ." The grim prospect of annihilation either by smallpox or the enemy had to be faced: "a large Fleet has arrived at Quebeck with 13,000 Regular Troops . . . we Just now hear that 10,000 of our enemies are landed on an Island oposit to Sorell about one mile distant . . . I am going to-

42

morrow to St. Johns to give directions to fortify there in order to Cover our Retreat, which I think must be soon without a miricle is rought in our favour."

Painter with Seth Warner's Rangers, too, had the task of covering the disorganized retreat from Canada, giving what support was possible to the ailing, and callous comfort to the dying.

Before the end of June 1776, Baldwin had arrived back at Crown Point and shortly received orders to Ticonderoga to perform the miracle of rebuilding the rundown fortifications, and Painter was among the hundreds of carpenters, masons, smiths, and lumberjacks employed in the task. Colonel Baldwin had a formidable assignment and a formidable capacity for accomplishment. For a year he supervised much of the military construction in the vicinity of Ticonderoga. His was a job of repairing vessels and building sawmills, constructing roads and mounting artillery, cutting timber and moving supplies, rigging ships and planning redoubts, locating encampments and building hospitals, constructing smith shops, blockhouses, laboratories, stores, ingenious hoists, platforms, batteries. He carried in his head the details as well as the general plans, and in the absence of a quartermaster made up the payrolls amounting each month to thousands of dollars. It was he who proposed building the first bridge across lower Lake Champlain and he who engineered the building of it in a matter of days. "I have," he wrote in his diary, "the intire direction of all the House & Ship Carpenters, the Smith, Armourers, Roap makers, the Wheel & Carriage makers, Miners, Turners, Coalyers, Sawyers & Shingle makers which are all togeather 286, besides the direction of all the fateagueing parties, so that I have my hands & mind constantly employed

43

night & Day except when I am a Sleep & Then sometimes I dream."

The Colonel could have chosen no better assistant than Gamaliel Painter, and Painter proved himself such an indefatigable laborer and competent artisan that he was later selected as Captain of the first company of Baldwin's Artificers. The two had much in common: a genius for getting from their charges maximum labor for minimum recompense, cool competence in any crisis, manual dexterity, a craft and skill at finding a practical substitute for an unavailable necessity.

But Painter had concerns in an assortment of other fields —concern for his family in Middlebury, concern for the political welfare of the Grants, concern for his brother. And the Declaration of Independence on July 4, 1776 stirred up new complications for all his interests. Realizing the seriousness of the situation on Lake Champlain, the Continental Congress on the day following the Declaration resolved that a Continental Regiment be raised out of the officers who had served with credit in the last campaign in Canada. The resolution stipulated that Seth Warner be the Colonel in charge, Elisha Painter a Major, and Gamaliel a First Lieutenant, their commissions to be withheld until the full complement was raised. In all, a list of some twenty officers was chosen from among those who had distinguished themselves in Canada, and there were already almost enough privates to fill the complement. There was little complaint about most of the officers Congress had designated, except for Elisha. The indignation that immediately arose over his appointment threatened to break up the entire remnant of the Green Mountain Boys. In Elisha they saw another Ethan Allen serving as third in command, a relative newcomer from Connecticut, a braggart who would

44

revive the pattern they had once rid themselves of in voting down Allen. For the first time mutiny came to their ranks.

Completely thwarted by Elisha's insistence that he was entitled to his commission, Warner was obliged to dispatch a letter to the Continental Congress, explaining that he could "find but two Captains of the late appointment, and but one of the former, who could serve under Elisha Painter, Esq. . . . The Captains in question are remarkably popular, and have great influence with the men many of them have commanded. With their assistance, a regiment would in all probability be readily completed. Without them, nothing to purpose can be expected."

Weeks of delay in recruiting the new regiment dragged on into months while Elisha refused to give up his commission. Gamaliel was unspeakably mortified that his brother would create such a stalemate. And it was not until Congress ordered Elisha in person "to repair to the city of Philadelphia, that the matter may be inquired into" that Warner was able to bring his recalcitrant captains to terms, and proceed with the formation of his regiment.

All the time that the wrangling was going on, it was anticipated that the redcoats might sweep down from the north any day to lay the Lake settlements in ruins. Gamaliel, worried about the safety of his family, took leave to look in at his neglected household and assist them in preparations for a hurried retreat to Connecticut when it became necessary. More cautious settlers were burying their highboys and spinning wheels in the woods, packing their ox carts, keeping the cattle in close tether and worrying about what, if any, government they were accountable to.

The Declaration of Independence had left the Painters

and settlers of their persuasion in an anomalous situation. The Grants for which they had paid New Hampshire were recognized even by the Continental Congress to be under the jurisdiction of New York. The British Crown had been petitioned for redress and there was reason to believe that the petition eventually would have received favorable response, but now all connection between Britain and the two contending colonies was broken and there remained no earthly power to which they could appeal for a decision on the controversy. The only logical step the Grant holders could now take was a bold declaration of their own independence, and in less than three weeks after Thomas Jefferson's document was announced to the world, Gamaliel Painter was seated in Kent's Tavern in Dorset arguing in favor of taking that step.

He reached Dorset, however, only by virtue of his good luck and his quick wit. Passing through Clarendon en route, he was suddenly ambushed by a posse of Tories who made their headquarters in that settlement. Had they recognized him, he would have made quarry in Albany worth at least half as much as Colonel Seth Warner. Painter knew Clarendon well: the Green Mountain Boys had made frequent excursions there to administer their form of justice to New York adherents; houses had been burned, roofs demolished and citizens given their quota of two hundred lashes on the bare back. He was at their mercy now; but unwaveringly he rode into their midst, and putting up a pretense of urgent haste informed them that he had no time to answer their questions and demanded that he be directed by the shortest route to the residence of Benjamin Spencer, a New York Justice of the Peace, and the most notorious leader of the Yorkers in the district. Three years before, the Green Mountain Boys had

46

subjected Spencer to a humiliating trial and passed sentence that his house be burned to the ground, but they had yielded to his entreaty and his persistent promises to change his allegiance, and finally compromised by tearing off the shingles and rafters of his roof with the understanding that when the house was restored, it would be in the name of New Hampshire. Spencer happened to reside in the south end of Clarendon, and having received explicit directions on where to find him, Gamaliel galloped off to Dorset.

To settle the account with malefactors like those at Clarendon, as well as their peers in New York, the Dorset Convention drafted the warning resolution "to take suitable measures, as soon as may be, to declare the New Hampshire Grants a free and separate district." They added patriotically that it was "absolutely necessary that every individual in the United States of America should exert themselves to the utmost of their abilities in the defense of the liberties thereof." Gamaliel and other members of the Committees of Safety had threatened before. They meant business now, and after circulating copies of the resolution east and west of the mountains, returned two months later to ratify it unanimously. And the "suitable measures" were taken the following January of 1777 when another convention at Westminster unequivocally declared the New Hampshire Grants "forever hereafter to be considered as a free and independent jurisdiction or state; by the name, and forever hereafter to be called, known and distinguished by the name of New Connecticut, alias Vermont."

Gamaliel was not present at the Westminster convention; there was no representative from Middlebury. The inhabitants were too occupied with plans for retreat and plans for the defense of sprawling Ticonderoga. The versatile Gamaliel had been detailed to intelligence duty, spying on the British crews which were surreptitiously invading the southern waters of Champlain. For this assignment he was cast as a halfwit salesman of tarts from Abigail's scant larder, a dispenser of eggs, cheese and such sweets as could be sacrificed from the diminishing supplies of diminishing settlers. And in the role he barely missed identification and the prospect of months or years in a Quebec dungeon. Dressed in the tattered homespun garb of a settler in the last throes of poverty, he appeared on the lake shore with a wicker basket on his arm and offered his wares for sale to the British patrol. Painter was promptly arrested and thrown into a small boat. He recovered his parcels, rearranged them preciously in his basket, and with the hurt pride of the idiot, calmly took inventory: "Six pieces of butter at three pence will bring a shilling and six pence for Mother. The eggs, Susie's eggs, dear Sister Susie, a dozen at a penny a piece make a shilling for Susie."

Peering over his shoulder he noted that the boat was closing in on a vessel at anchor in the Lake, where he could anticipate an examination that would quickly strip him of his pose. Quite unconcerned he continued with his inane patter of Susie, Mother, eggs, cheese, and tarts. "This fellow is a perfect idiot," ventured one of the officers. "We should be ashamed to take him up there." The course of the boat was changed, and Painter was shortly delivered to more appreciative customers of his wares.

He returned to Ticonderoga where he resumed his dignity as an officer and vowed that he had served his last duty as a spy. Thousands of men were now working frantically at the Fort. Attack had been delayed by the magnificent conflagra-

48

tion of a naval store and provision magazine at St. Johns, but reliable intelligence now revealed that the British were on their way. Colonel Baldwin was everywhere at once, putting the finishing touches on the clumsy floating bridge, mounting cannon, strengthening the fortifications on Mount Independence, and complacently ignoring Mount Defiance, an adjacent eminence which rose six hundred feet higher, with cliffs which appeared far too sheer for any artillery unit to ascend. But Painter had to beg for leave when the excitement of preparations was at its climax. A convention had been called to draft a constitution for the republic of Vermont and, despite the critical situation at Ticonderoga, this legislative event was more important to Painter than imminent military events.

Lieutenant Painter made the trip to Windsor and helped to frame the noble document, but in his enthusiasm for lawmaking, he missed the capitulation of the Fort. On July 2, 1777, the British landed their troops and started the siege, and to the amazement of the frontiersmen, the artillery readily dragged cannon to the top of Mount Defiance, making it obvious to the lowliest American private that the enemy had strategic control. There was no choice left but complete and immediate evacuation. The months of work that had gone into repairing the rotting bastion, the thousands of tedious hours spent in constructing wharves, storehouses, barracks, batteries, breastworks and the ingenious pontoon bridge proved a total loss in a matter of hours. On the night of July 5, illuminated by a full moon and a fire imprudently set on Mount Independence, some 3000 Continentals and volunteers quietly retreated to Vermont across Colonel Baldwin's bridge. The Colonel, without reference to calamity, and to the end, solicitous of the success of his contributions, casually noted in his diary: "about 10 o'clock at night a Speedy retreat was ordered and the main boddy of the army got off From Ty & Mount Independence a little before Sunrise followed by the Enemy but did but little damage."

Painter learned of the imminent fiasco on the afternoon of July 2 while perspiring with the other delegates over constitutional phraseology. He was among those who would have abandoned the convention without adopting a constitution had it not been for a violent thunderstorm which suddenly broke over Windsor simultaneously with the news. The storm necessarily kept the delegates in session through the afternoon, and the document by which the new Republic existed was given birth in a violence of deluge, thunder and lightning:

> Whereas, all government ought to be instituted and supported, for the security and protection of the community, . . . And whereas, the inhabitants of this State have, (in consideration of protection only) heretofore acknowledged allegiance to the King of Great Britain, and the said King has not only withdrawn that protection, but commenced . . . a most cruel and unjust war, . . . And whereas, the territory which now comprehends the State of Vermont, did antecedently, of right, belong to the government of New-Hampshire; . . . And whereas the late Lieutenant Governor . . . did, in violation of the tenth command, covet those very lands . . . they have sent the savage on our frontiers, to distress us . . . And whereas, the local situation of this State, from New York, at the extreme part, is upward of four hundred and fifty miles from the seat of that government, . . . Therefore, it is absolutely necessary, for the welfare and safety of the inhabitants of this state, that it should be, henceforth, a free and independent State; and that a just, permanent and proper form of government, should exist in it, derived from, and founded on, the authority of the people only . . .

Four days after the adoption of the Constitution, on the retreat from Ticonderoga toward Castleton, Seth Warner's regiment was temporarily decimated at the breakfast battle of Hubbardton, the only Revolutionary battle fought on Vermont soil. Lieutenant Painter never fought again with his Green Mountain Boys. After the fall of Ticonderoga, the Champlain Valley was wide open to the depredations of British, Tories, and their Indian allies. They swept in, pillaging every semblance of settlement in their path. Painter took advantage of the military chaos to escort his family to the safety of Connecticut.

3 ARTIFICER

Gamaliel had as much in common with his brother Elisha as the tolerant lawyer Gamaliel of the New Testament had with the irrepressible prophet Elisha of the Old. All the ancestral family traits of the waterfront Painters, with their indifference to proprieties, rested with Elisha. He was a swaggering fighter who would sooner give argument or give battle than indulge in any security or refinements of the home front. He had taken a pitch in Panton, a pitch in Middlebury, a wife and a farm in Connecticut, but had been attentive to none of them. The greatest satisfaction he knew was in the thick of a good brawl or on the march to some new catastrophe. He had found that sort of satisfaction at Ticonderoga

53

and in Canada. He did not find it in Philadelphia where he was summoned after being disowned by the Green Mountain Boys.

At the capital city he pled his case for reinstatement with a persistence and self-assurance that would have done honor to his idol Ethan Allen. He talked and wrote eloquently of his "faithful and arduous services," his devotion to the "darling cause" and the "unnatural war." He proclaimed his ignorance of anything he had done to promote "uneasiness and dissatisfaction" among Colonel Warner's men. He even managed to secure from one officer who had served under him a clean bill of health certifying that Elisha never used bad language, never indulged in "hard drinking, gaming or night routs," and never set a bad example for his men.

But the pleas were convincing neither to Congress nor to the Board of War. By the first of the year 1777, the Continental Congress was able to put aside more pressing legislative obligations and resolve "That the said Elisha Painter be removed from any warrant in the said regiment, and be referred to General Washington for an appointment to such an office as he shall judge him qualified to fill." But even this rebuke from the highest authority on the North American continent did not settle Elisha's ire. He stayed on in Philadelphia to sulk, fume and lobby. Washington was unable immediately to find a billet suitable to his talents, and four months later the Continental Congress was called upon to hear a second verbose appeal from the irresponsible Major. Elisha had found sympathetic supporters and political patrons in the right quarter. The appeal was passed through channels from Congress to the Board of War, and in three days a report came back that the complaint against Major Painter

54

was completely without foundation. Congress, however, was not ready to offer the same kind of unqualified exoneration. It warily adopted a resolution that he be allowed to return to his command, "unless Washington shall think proper to appoint him to some other office or employment in the army." Washington obviously did not think it proper to send him back to Vermont. He immediately gave him a temporary appointment as superintendent of Artificers at his Morristown Headquarters where he could keep him under observation.

Throughout the months that the controversy between Elisha and the Continental Congress dragged on, Gamaliel suffered the starkest humiliation. Inevitably the censure of Elisha was transferred to Gamaliel. He had always been over-shadowed and dominated by his brother; now he had been innocently subjected to indignity and disgrace because of the relationship, and lost favor with his own men. When Elisha was finally withdrawn from Warner's Regiment, Gamaliel followed the only course his shy self-respect would allow, and rejected his own Lieutenancy. But as soon as Colonel Jeduthan Baldwin and Udny Hay, Assistant Deputy Quartermaster General, who had been closely associated with Painter in Canada, heard of it, Gamaliel was offered a raise in rank and a commission as the first captain in a newly organized Regiment of Artificers. By accident Elisha had also become an Artificer, but he was far enough removed so that there was slim likelihood of their immediately crossing each other's paths. Gamaliel accepted his commission and was ordered to set about recruiting his own company.

The Artificers were the elite among the entire roster of the Continental and Provincial armies. The officers represented the shrewdest soldiers and sharpest marksmen in the service, but craftsmanship rather than belligerence identified the Artificers. In addition to prowess at arms, each Artificer had to qualify as an expert in some craft essential to organized warfare, such as carpentry, gunsmithing, rope-making, blacksmithing, tailoring, baking, road building. A company of Artificers was expected to furnish proficient artisans to manufacture or repair anything that a raw private or brigadier general might need at a given moment, and be prepared on short notice to serve as aggressive vanguard for a marching army in need of bridge builders, woodsmen, scouts and repairmen. What they lacked as a group in military bearing they readily made up in dexterity. And out of respect for their talents and temperament, they were accorded privileges which officers of rank in the infantry or cavalry seldom acquired.

Washington had employed Artificers in the French and Indian Wars with notable success, and one of his first demands upon acceptance of his appointment as Commander-in-Chief was that provision be made for them in the Continental Army. As early as September 1775 he had warned the Continental Congress that a dissolution of the Army could be expected if, among other necessities, provision were not made for "the Pay of Artificers, distinct from that of Common Soldiers." Washington proceeded to recruit his artisans, though authority for it was not granted until late in the year when an unenthusiastic resolution was finally voted "that this Congress approve the terms on which the Artificers of different sorts have been employed . . . as being the best that can probably be made." The terms included one "suite of cloths," a special ration of a pound and a half of bread or flour per day, a pound and a half of meat, and a daily libation of a pint of rum.

Without much formal order, the Artificers had been tried out in Canada and New York under Jeduthan Baldwin, but it was not until December 1776, after Colonel Henry Knox in a personal memorandum to Washington had proposed attaching a company of Artificers to the field artillery, that they began to take on a semblance of organization. Knox maintained that only "the best men should be employed in this service" and that their pay should be "twenty-five P cent more than the marching regiments."

Washington was so gratified to discover a practical field officer interested in the Artificers that Knox was retroactively promoted to the rank of Brigadier General, not to the date he accomplished the all but impossible feat of conducting an army across the ice-filled Delaware but to the date of his memorandum, and, following Knox's recommendation, on January 16, 1777 the Commander-in-Chief outlined his conception of a well-balanced company of Artificers: "One Master Carpenter, One Master Wheelwright and One Master Blacksmith, two Tinmen, two Turners, two Coopers, Four Harness Makers, two Nailers, and Two Farriers, Six Wheelwrights, Twenty five Carpenters and Fifteen Smiths, the Whole being Sixty, under the direction of a Master Carpenter."

Gamaliel Painter qualified as a Master Carpenter and as one of the best men in the service to whom Knox had referred. His commission was dated July 21, 1777, and as soon as he had restored his family to the relative security of Connecticut, he set about the task of recruiting his company. He was now privileged to wear the most distinguished regalia in the Army. Whereas most of the regulars had simple blue uniforms faced with white and decorated with white buttons, Captain Painter of the Artificers had an impressive blue outfit faced and lined with scarlet and dotted with yellow buttons. His coat was edged with a fine lace, his waistcoat was red, and his hat handsomely bound in gold. In it Gamaliel looked as conspicuous as he felt. But it was a uniform that commanded respect and admiration, if not reverence, in any circle. It entitled the wearer to the best available quarters and the best available food.

Dressed in this spectacular garb and attended by a Lieutenant or Sergeant, he rode back and forth, up and down the southwestern counties of Connecticut combing the manufacturing towns for a carpenter or blacksmith, saddler or tinsmith, wheelwright or gunsmith, tailor or tent maker. He covered the shore towns from Milford and New Haven to Saybrook and New London. He followed up the Thames to swear in two recruits at Norwich and others in the nearby villages of Colchester and Lebanon; then westward to the region of Hartford to find a scattering of candidates at Farmington and Glastonbury; again down the Connecticut River to Middletown and the Haddams, and all the way west to Danbury, Woodbury and Litchfield. It took from the first of August until the middle of the following April to assemble a full company.

Gamaliel was a poor salesman, and the territory had already been worked over time and again by more able spokesmen for the cause of battle than he. The men he wanted were hard to come by. They were the pillars of their communities, and the life of the community was as dependent in wartime on cobblers and coopers, smiths and saddlers, as it was in peacetime. They were apt to be better artisans than warriors. Most of them had dependent families, and the wives and daughters of mechanics could not carry on shopwork in their absence as easily as wives and daughters of common soldiers could keep up the farms.

To each new non-commissioned officer or soldier he was authorized to offer an enticement of twenty dollars along with "two linnen Hunting-Shirts, Two pair of hose, Two pair of Overhalls, A leathern or woolen Waistcoat with sleeves, One pair of Breeches, One Hat or leathern cap, and Two pair of Shoes. Amounting in the whole to the value of Twenty Dollars more." But even with these inducements, and the pledge of higher wages, better rations, more rum and the final promise of a hundred acres of land at the end of the war, Captain Painter's recruiting progressed slowly.

Then it was necessary to follow the meticulous instructions issued to recruiting officers "to be careful to enlist none but healthy able-bodied Men who shall engage to serve in the army of the United States of America during the present war or for the term of three years." He was required to register "the age, size, complexion, colour of hair and eyes, and natural and accidental mark of every Recruit, with an account of the place of his birth and occupation," and finally to administer the oath of allegiance before a local Justice of the Peace or Chief Magistrate.

In his role as an officer in the Continental Army, Painter discovered that he was required to enforce a kind of rigorous discipline, the like of which he had never been exposed to under either Ethan Allen or Seth Warner. With the Green Mountain Boys, personal affairs had often taken precedence over military affairs, and one dropped out of his unit as his conscience or his wife dictated; the organization had been largely on a voluntary basis, but with the Continentals there was no such informality. Enlistment meant regimentation

59

and total loss of alternative. Threat of court-martial was ever present among the liberty-loving and free-speaking troops. The slightest word of disrespect for a superior officer "tending to his hurt or dishonor" was a court-martial offense, as was "any reproachful or provoking speeches or gesture to another." Absence from troops or company was a grave offense, and any soldier "found one mile from the camp without leave in writing," or any soldier who chose to "lie out of his quarters or camp without leave" could expect a regimental court-martial. An officer caught drunk on duty was dismissed from the service with ignominy, a far cry from some of the celebrations in which Painter had participated on the shores of Lake Champlain. To be sure, liquor was considered a military necessity and was freely rationed when it was available, but no sutler was "permitted to sell any kind of liquor or victuals, or to keep his house or shop open for the entertainment of soldiers, after nine at night, or before the beating of reveilles, or upon Sundays, during divine service or sermon."

The earnest recommendation that officers and soldiers "diligently attend Divine service" was virtually a requirement, and the wrath of military judgment awaited any who behaved "indecently or irreverently at any place of Divine Worship." Even swearing, such as Colonel Commandant Ethan Allen cultivated among the Green Mountain Boys, now brought serious punishment, with a fine of one sixth of a dollar for the first "profane oath or execration"; a twenty-four hour confinement and another sixth of a dollar for a second. And if a commissioned officer were found guilty of "profane cursing or swearing," he forfeited and paid "for each and every such offence the sum of Four shillings, legal money."

As an overbearing disciplinarian, Painter was far from adequate, but before Washington's dejected encampment at Valley Forge had thawed out in the Spring of 1778, the Captain of the Artificers was ready to march his raw, soft-spoken Connecticut recruits south to Pennsylvania and expose them to more ordered indoctrination at Headquarters. The period of training, however, was of short duration, for when the British finally decided to call an end to their winter of debauchery in Philadelphia and to retreat north before anticipated French reinforcements arrived to bolster the rebel cause, Painter's Company was among those ordered into action to slow the march of the enemy and harass him at every opportunity.

Specifically the Artificers were given the task of facilitating the movements of the infantry, rebuilding bridges, repairing equipment, making roads passable. "There will be a party of Artificers to go in front and rear of the whole, to mend Bridges and repair the Broken Carriages," Washington ordered on June 18, 1778, adding that they would be supported by "a party of Pioneers to move in front of the Columns, to assist the Artificers in repairing Bridges and bad places in the roads." Under this directive Painter's Artificers became involved in one of the major battles of the Revolution: Monmouth.

It was probably at Valley Forge, prior to Monmouth, that Painter took the new oath of allegiance as required of all commissioned officers by resolution of Congress: "I, Gamaliel Painter, do acknowledge the United States of America to be free, independent and sovereign States, and declare that the people thereof owe no allegiance or obedience to George the Third, King of Great Britain; and I . . . will serve the said United States in the office of Captain which I now hold, with

61

fidelity, according to the best of my skill and understanding. So help me God."

Painter could take the oath without reservation, but Major General Charles Lee, on whom the Monmouth engagement hinged, openly expressed reservation, the true meaning of which did not come to light until after the baggage train of the fleeing British had advanced nine days north, to the vicinity of Monmouth, a procession nearly twelve miles long, "all the soldiers of Clinton's army, foot, horse and artillery, provision train, baggage, army wagons, numerous private carriages, a large number of bat-horses, bakeries, launderies, and blacksmith shops on wheels, large hospital supplies, boats, bridges, magazines, withal a crowd of female camp followers and every kind of useless stuff."

On the 28th of June, Washington gave orders to Lee to engage the enemy with the five thousand men under him. Confused and cowed by his conception of the size and strength of the opposing forces, the Major General virtually disregarded the orders, and was forced to retreat in confusion until Washington personally took command and salvaged the situation. "Never," commented Lafayette, "was General Washington greater in war than in this action. His presence stopped the retreat; his dispositions fixed the victory; his fine appearance on horseback, his calm courage roused to animation by the vexations of the morning gave him the air best calculated to excite enthusiasm . . . He rode along the lines, amid the shouts of the soldiers, cheering them by his voice and example and restoring to our standard the fortunes of the fight." This was the leader that Captain Painter saw in action.

But Lee's vacillation caused an inordinate amount of labor for the Artificers in repairing artillery carriages, laying makeshift roads, rebuilding crossings over ravines and rivers, and throwing up barriers and entrenchments. "Intrenching tools are to be assigned to the brigades in due proportion, and delivered to the care of the Brigade Quartermaster," ordered the Commander-in-Chief. "When circumstances will permit, the artificers and pioneers will advance before the van-guard of the Army and repair the roads with fascines and earth, instead of rails, which serve to cripple the horses."

Painter's home-trained Artificers won their share of laurels during the eventful day. They demonstrated that civilian ingenuity could be as effective in the field of battle as military engineering. The American infantry stood against the formidable British bayonet charges. The Artillery matched the batteries of Britain. Barricaded behind nothing more substantial than hedges and rail fences, they faced the onslaught, held their ground, and repulsed the enemy. Once and for all, the Continentals convinced both themselves and the British that the military school of Valley Forge was a magnificent success. Monmouth was a major victory for the Americans, the first victory in which the Continental line vanquished the best troops of Great Britain. The American patriots proved that they had the technique as well as the spirit to cope with soldiers who were "clearly superior to any fighting men in the world at the time." "To defeat such soldiers . . . , to cause such men to abandon the battlefield was glory enough for any army."

But what battlefield glory Painter won at Monmouth was his last. His combat career ended as abruptly as it began. He did not participate in another battle during the entire Revolution. His Artificers were needed more behind the lines than in them. With the victorious army he tramped back to New York, but his company was soon sent to the Highlands on the Hudson to carry on the multifarious chores of Artificers in the vital encampment at Fishkill, where Washington was setting up further winter headquarters and a major depot for provisions.

Located five miles east of the Hudson and some fifteen miles north of West Point, Fishkill was on the main highway to Connecticut and to the manufacturing towns of New England; it was on the route up and down the Hudson which the British still hoped to cut; it commanded the Wiccopee Pass, "a narrow defile immediately south of the village which might easily be held by a small army against a much larger attacking force," and through which any invaders would have to pass. The town had little to offer except a rugged mountain setting, Dutch churches converted to military use, and a few dozen pioneer homes spread over a wide area; but against the mountains, a grim, disordered army city had sprung up with extensive barracks, hospitals, workshops, magazines, prisons, and hundreds of windowless stone huts which men and officers alike were privileged to build for themselves, if stationed there long enough to warrant summoning dependent members of the family. The huts were built in almost identical fashion of native stone, chinked with clay and heated by a scant fireplace which was little more than a recess in the wall next to the door, "a miserable shelter for the severe weather of this country," wrote one observer, ". . . little walls made with uneven stones, and the intervals filled up with mud and straw, a few planks forming the roof."

Painter became a member of the hungry, chaotic community, and into one of these huts he moved his family, as ragged and penniless as the other army followers. The countryside offered poor fare for the most persistent scavenger. Even firewood had to be drawn on hand sleds by individual occupants of the huts. A sack of flour or a pair of shoes now cost close to a hundred dollars, but fortunately Salisbury was less than forty miles across the hills, and the steady flow of traffic from Connecticut brought occasional help from friends to supplement the starvation rations.

The Captain had long since worn through his showy uniform and was reduced to whatever garments he could procure for warmth or covering. He was a laborer and a leader of other laborers. To the Artificers came orders to cut forests, to construct highways, and build barracks. To the Artificers came orders to repair rifles, shoes and saddles. To the Artificers came urgent orders to locate or commandeer provisions, equipment and raw material which no other department was succesful in securing. Painter's company was called upon for auxiliary services at Hartford, White Plains, Middlebrook, Morristown. There were latrines to be built at White Plains, lumber to be cut in the Catskills, bridges to be repaired on the road south from King's Ferry to New Jersey. There was gruelling, fatiguing work, and monotonous, enervating drudgery. Long days and nights of uninterrupted manual labor were followed by days of dull military routine.

Artificers were needed wherever there were troops, but they could not be everywhere at once. It was next to impossible for any Commander to keep his specialists employed in the place where they were most needed. The American army was so dispersed that officers were constantly calling upon Washington for the recruitment of more Artificers, when there were unemployed Artificers in remote encampments. "The number of applications for manufacturers and artificers of different

65

kinds, could they all be complied with, would be a considerable loss to the army," replied Washington annoyed by the recurrent appeal. Or again, with less patience, "The draughts for the Army, for Teamsters, Mechanics, and persons of different occupations are so great, that our return upon command, amounts to almost half the effective fit for duty."

The mechanics were more used to giving orders than taking orders. They were used to staying put in their shops, resented being shipped from place to place, and with minimum exposure to military discipline, unhesitatingly expressed their indifference to orders. The alternate monotony and severity of the labor played havoc with morale among the Artificers at Fishkill. And, worst of all, the promises of special favors failed to materialize. There was so much dissatisfaction with wages, so much dissatisfaction with rations, so much dissatisfaction with commanding officers that Washington was forced to order the Quartermaster General "to make an inquiry into the disturbance among the Artificers," and to demand that they were not to be slighted in their special rations of "1½ lb Bread or Flour, 1½ lb. Meat, and half a pint of Rum pr. day," with the emphasis on the Rum. So many of the Artificers continued to appeal for reassignment to other regiments where work, meals and compensation were more regular, that Washington had to issue special orders to West Point: "They must be paid in Rum (if that was the agreement) or an equivalent in Money when they do not get Rum. They must not at any Rate think of returning to their Regiments while their services are wanting."

And as though Painter did not have his share of concerns and worries with his men and his family, hardly had he become established at Fishkill when Elisha was ordered to nearby West Point, and his headstrong brother was in trouble

66

again. Gamaliel was due to suffer new humiliation more smarting to his pride than his previous experience. "At a General Court Martial held at West Point, Sept. 28, 1778 . . .," Gamaliel read in the General Orders, "Elisha Painter, Major of Artificers was tried for absenting himself from the Garrison and neglect of duty, found guilty of the charges exhibited against him and sentenced to be dismissed the service."

On the very day Elisha received the sentence, his indignation burst forth in a seething letter of protest written directly to the Commander-in-Chief. He avowed that this absence for which he had been called to task was covered by a "liberty and Pass" for an indefinite period to collect "money, Blankets & Cloathing" for his suffering men. "I have done nothing with Intention to Rong, Injure, or Defraud the United States, or to disobey & break any Orders, Rules or Regulations thereof . . . After all my Sufferings in Person and Property, . . . to be turned out in a Scandalous (and as I view it) Unjust maner, is too much for an Honest Hearted friend to American Liberty to Indure . . . Being discharged the Service in a maner Degrading, Is very mortifying to me who have ben a faithfull Servant and Friend to it. Especially as I am Conscious of my Innocence in the Afair, and that I am not Guilty . . ."

Elisha maintained that he had been tried by a Court Martial composed of officers of subordinate rank, and demanded a retrial. With sixteen other officers, Gamaliel dutifully signed an endorsement of the appeal. Washington recognized the technical error and patiently ordered that Major Painter be given a new trial, adding slyly: "He can have no occasion to complain again should his sentence be the same."

Then, for over a year, the case remained unsettled, while

various Commands argued over where he should be tried and by whom. Elisha was taken desperately ill and appealed to General Arnold for permission to be taken to the seaside because he was "unable to attend to the Business of Said tryal" and did not expect "for a long while to be able to attend to any kind of Business." But the retrial was never held. On January 12, 1781, he called in witnesses and solemnly made out his will:

> In the name of God, Amen . . . I Elisha Painter . . . being Ill as to bodily State, but of sound disposing Mind and Memory, & not knowing but that great changes may be nearly approaching & being desirous to dispose of my worldly Interests, before my Death, have devised & ordained this my last Will and Testament, in Manner and Form following: that is to say, above all, committing my Soul into ye hands of my blessed Sav^r, & recommending my Body to ye Dust, to be decently interr^d and as touching my worldly Estate . . . I will & bequeath to my well beloved Wife Hannah ye whole of my moveable Estate . . . As to my real Estate . . . it be divided between my beloved Wife Hannah Painter & my Brother Gamaliel Painter and my sisters . . .

The next day he died as stealthily and as mysteriously as he had lived, and though he had frequently indicated he was a man of property, the inventory of the estate showed that he was virtually a pauper—nineteen acres of land in Middlebury, three acres in New Haven, a "fether reed", an old coat, "a pair of breaches", "a Block Chains", "a trammel", "a pair of handdionns", a plow, an old chest, an iron pot, a "Great chair"—all valued at less than fifty-five pounds. His wife was left destitute, and Hannah's humble appeals to the General Assembly of the State of Connecticut for "consideration of her unfortunate circumstances" fell on as deaf ears as had her husband's appeals to the Commander-in-Chief.

68

Meantime Captain Painter had on his hands a hopelessly demoralized group of officers and men. The gruesome picture was presented by the Board of War to the Continental Congress in a desperate appeal for relief:

> Their difficulties daily increase . . . The officers, already deeply distressed, will not continue in the Service to their *certain ruin* . . . The officers in the regiment who do the double duty of superintending their own men & those hired to assist them, complain that they see themselves and families reduced to want . . . The inlisted artificers draw very grating comparisons between their own & the situation of hired men, who have ten times their pay.
>
> The condition of these people is peculiar, as most of them have families with whom they connected themselves either previous to their inlistment or Since their engaging in the corps, which being Stationary induces them to enter into matrimonial engagements more than the men in the marching regiments. The families of such men are distressed, and themselves discontented . . . their pay, from the depreciation of currency, is trifling . . .
>
> The officers of the regiment of artillery artificers could, by resigning, resume their Several employments to great advantage; as most of them, before they entered into the public Service, were Master Workmen, possessed of considerable property . . .
>
> We know that many of our officers complain that their pay is not equal to that of a common artificer: but they do not advert to the difference of their Situations. The military officer has promotion and glory for his objects, but the artificer has only his wages to invite him to his duty. For these reasons we think that no bad precedent will be established by raising the pay of the artificers . . .

For two months Painter waited anxiously for the reply which he felt certain would bring some sort of solace, but when the reply came it was as melancholy as the despondency in which he lived. The pay could not be raised; Congress was receiving demands on every hand for relief from the currency depreciation; the Artificers could not be singled out for further special favors, and they slowly disintegrated at a time when their services were most needed. Painter disconsolately applied for a discharge, but it was rejected.

At Fishkill, he was existing with his family in abject poverty. Finally, in despair, he buried his pride and addressed a pitiful letter to Major General Benedict Arnold:

Fish Kill Landing, 9th Sept. 1780

Honored Sir

I hope I have not troubled you in the Epistolary way that your Honour will Spend one thought on the subject of this—I took an active part on the American Side at the time your Honour took Ticonderoga in the Year 1775—in the Year 1776 when our Army Retreated from Canada, I was obliged to Quit my Home, or be under British Government, as I Lived 12 Miles East of Crown point, and have had my Family on Expense ever Since—21st July 1777 I had ordered to Recruit a Company of Artificers, which I did & have the Command of them now. the pay has been so frivolous and to help along Connecticut Assembly has Refused to make up the Depreciation of the Artificers wages—all my Misfortunes put together, has reduced me to the Necessity of Bringing my Family to Fish Kill, Expecting to draw Some provisions for them, as I under Stood that it was tolerated—but Col⁰ Hay whose Direction I have been under, Gives me to understand that it is not his province to give any Liberty that way—Honoured Sir if it is Consistent Either by the Custom of the army, or, my Needy Circumstances, to give an order to Draw provisions for my wife and two Boys (the oldest of which is in his twelvth Year) as I am ordered to Camp, and have no money to buy, and to beg I am Ashamed—it will in Some Measure Relieve the Needy and Much Oblige—Honoured Sir Your Devoted & Most Humble Servt

Gam¹ Painter

Maj Genl Arnold.

Despite the unorthodox nature of the letter, Painter forwarded it through proper channels to the Assistant Deputy Quartermaster General, Major William M. Betts at Peekskill, and the Major was sufficiently touched by the genuineness of the appeal and the record of his Captain to attach an endorsement, and send it along, without too much optimism that it would have any more chance of being honored than had innumerable other more general and more official appeals:

> I wou^d just beg leave to mention that if any indulgence of that Kind cou^d be granted, Capt Painters Merrits and situation might justly claim your attention as he has on all occasions conducted as a faithful and Active Servant to the public and is justly esteem^d a Valuable Officer.

To the amazement of Major Betts and the Commissary, three days later came a note from General Arnold's aide, Richard Varick, granting to Painter what had been refused other applicants:

> I am directed by Major General Arnold to acknowledge the receipt of, and answer, your letters of the 9th and 10th.
> Captain Painter's request, supported by your commendation, is complied with, and for that purpose I do inclose you an order in his favor. Please to fill in the Commissary's as well as Mr Painter's Names. I suppose him absent and do not answer his letter . . .

Painter was on his way to a new temporary assignment at Camp Tottawa by the time the relief came to his family, but he would readily have given up the subsistence benefits and no longer been ashamed to beg for his family when he learned ten days later that his benefactor Arnold had been exposed as a traitor, plotting with the young Frenchman, André, to surrender West Point to the British, a calamity which could have turned the American Revolution into a British victory.

As one who had been singled out for special consideration by the traitor, Painter's whole war record inevitably underwent the closest scrutiny. It meant reviving the details of charges against his brother as they might throw light on Gamaliel; it meant an investigation of his relations with his superior, Colonel Udny Hay, who, with members of his family, was virtually banished from Fishkill under suspicion of complicity. Painter's mortification at becoming involved again in suspicious circumstances of which he had had no part, embittered him for the rest of his military career. Under the closest scrutiny were his Connecticut background, his associations and conduct in Middlebury, his participation in the Canadian expeditions, his record at Monmouth, the character of his recruits and the itinerary of his company. But by November he had been cleared of any charges of suspicion for he was back on temporary duty under the aegis of Washington at Camp Tottawa, and the Commander-in-Chief had decided to grant to all the families of artificers what had been granted to Painter's: "You will be pleased," he ordered Lt. Colonel Hay, "to supply those who have families, with a reasonable quantity of Meat, Flour, and Salt on account of their Wages."

All that Washington could do to keep his favored Artificers together during the closing months of the war, however, was too little. He encouraged the states to supplement their pay; he gave them a place of honor in parades; he demanded that rice be substituted for flour when bread was not available; he chided the Quartermaster because "not a drop of Rum has yet come on and the Physicians report that the Artificers (who labor exceedingly hard) are falling sick for want of it;" for special expeditions he ordered that new Artificers be paid an additional nine shillings and six pence per day; plans for their reorganization were drawn up, with Painter retained as Captain of the first company.

Largely on his own meager funds and in spare time Painter had converted one of the more dilapidated Fishkill huts into liveable quarters for his family, but upon his return from Tottawa he was greeted by a barracks officer with the information that his residence was needed by a superior officer. Painter seldom lost his temper, but being subjected to this sort of ignominy was more than he could tolerate. In the cause of his country, he had lost one home, had made himself destitute, and devoted his energies and ingenuity to the common struggle. With humility he could endure privations for himself, but he would not have his family deprived of the last vestige of animal comfort. In the heat of his fury, he sat down that night and drafted a blistering letter, not to the barracks officer, not to his C.O. at Fishkill or West Point, but to Colonel Pickering himself, Washington's Quartermaster General:

> Fish Kill Landing 28th Decr 1780
> Necessity alone Drives me to trouble Your Honour with this Epistle—
> I have had the misfortain of being a Refugee Since our Army Retreeted from Canada, and have had no Settled Place for my Famely Since, Last Spring I Saw no way but my Famely to Suffer if I Continued in the Service, In Consequence of which I applyed to Colo Hay to be Recommendad for a Discharge; he Gave me to understand that he had not long befor wrote a Letter to Genl Green which would interfear with any thing that he could write Reletive to my being discharge, but proposed for me to Bring my Famely to the House that I now Posess, (as it was emty,) I objected on account of there being only one Small Room and the Roof very Leaky, he Said it Should be made Comfortable for me, in

consequence of which I brought my Famely, but the Campaign opened and Col° Hay about to Quit the Department Put it out of his Power to give me the assistance that he expected, And to live in the House as it was I could not, which made me undertake to get it don as I could, I made a light Roof (the Shingles and Nailes was Public) and a addition of two Small Rooms about nine feet Square each, The Timber for which I Procured and Twenty Boards with the greatest Part of the Labour at my own expense (which I know of no way to obtain from the Public) Little thinking at that time that I Should have the Useage that I am about to Receive—

Last night as I was Returning from a tour that I had Proformed by Order of Col° Baldwin I was overtook by Mr Wilson who Said he was Assistant Barrack Master and Said he was Glad to Sea me as he was going to order Mrs Painter to be ready to move early in the Morning and that he had Perticular orders from Col° Pickering for that Purpose, and as I was come he Should Send the Teams for my Good, for answer I told him that he need not Send any Teams for I had no Use for them as I Designed to have a Place to live in before I Quit that, he Said he had a Place for me &c, which Place I have been to Sea but hope that there is no Authority that has a Right to Order me into that House even if I am Obliged to Quit this, The House has Two Rooms on a Floor with Cellar Kitchen in which one of the family Lives in Preference to the Room Design^d for me—They say no Family Shall come in as they have Hired the House and Think Two Family is Sufficiant to fill it—

Question whether a Man that Setts so little by his own Wellfare as to Suffer Himself to be turn^d out of a House that he has made comfortable (good part at his own Expence.) With the offer of going in to a House (if he can get the People that lives in it Willing) That in a Rainy day cannot keep himself Dry. Is a fit Person to help Support the liberty of America—

Honour^d Sir I have every Reason to think that You have not been made Acquainted with those matter, that I have here Relaited, Pray You^ll Spend one thought on my Situation, after which (having full confidence of Your cander and

Impartiality in those Matters) am willing to Submit my case
to your own feelings—

I am Sir
Most Respectfully
Your Most Obe[t]
Ser[t]
Gam[l] Painter

Col[o] Pickering

From an officer with little standing in the eyes of his su-
periors, such a letter could have merited a court martial for
the writer, with charges of insolence, insubordination, and
defiance of authority. Not so with Artificer Painter. Within
twenty-four hours Colonel Baldwin was directed to "remove
Capt. Painter and family to the Barracks as speedily as may
be, in Case there is a room vacant, and no better provision can
otherwise be made."

Others, however, did not fare as well. The morale of the
Artificers had deteriorated so critically that it was too late
to recondition them. Washington expressed his grave disap-
pointment and complained to Colonel Pickering, the Quartermaster General, that "Among the many things that demand
your particular attention and regulation, I know of none, that
in superficial view seems to do it more than the corps of
Artificers." Pickering countered by recommending that all except the Artillery Artificers be discharged, and by March 28,
1781, Washington and Congress were convinced that it was
the only plausible course of action, and concluded "that the
regiment of artificers, commanded by Colonel Baldwin, be
dissolved; and those of the non-commissioned officers and
privates whose times of service are unexpired, and are now
with the main army, be formed into one company . . . , that
all officers of the regiment of artificers not retained by virtue

75

of these resolutions, be no longer considered in the service of the United States."

Colonel Baldwin and most of his men and officers were forthwith released from service, and according to the voice of Congress, Captain Painter should have joined them; his company was disbanded, but as one of the indispensables he stayed on at Fishkill under the Quartermaster, along with the shoemakers and saddlers. To him fell the impossible assignment of requisitioning hides for "mending saddles, Making Shoes, and other work for the publick." He did the impossible and managed to haul to Fishkill from Connecticut a total of two hundred hides.

The State of Connecticut had at last been prevailed upon to furnish supplementary family supplies, so that Painter no longer was in extreme want; nevertheless he and other ex-officers of Colonel Baldwin's regiment opened up on the Continental Congress with a barrage of demands for subsidy in depreciated back pay. Painter's dispatch to Congress requested clarification as to "whether it was intended that they should be entitled to the same emoluments as officers in the line of the army." The query was referred to a committee and then to the Board of War, but Painter received small satisfaction. Congress recognized the fact that the Artificers were "in a very destitute situation and their minds being thereby embittered they are of consequence full of complaints and uneasyness," but the States would have to settle his question.

Painter spent the last weeks of his service in the same miscellaneous construction work on which he had labored during most of the years of the war; repairing boats, cutting lumber, rebuilding wagons, serving as mason, leather worker, carpenter, and wheelwright. On April 20, 1782, Washington issued the order that "No artificer from the line is to be retained by the Quarter Master of West Point, except he first obtain a certificate from the Commanding Officer of the Garrison that such an Artificer is absolutely requisite for such a particular purpose." Painter's services at last were no longer needed. Tired and destitute, he gathered his family together, and rode over the familiar Berkshire Hills back to Salisbury, Connecticut. He had no home in Vermont to which he could return.

4 FARMER

In all of the Middlebury region there were but four buildings
left standing after the war. Burgoyne's demolition scouts had
done a thorough job, though they had somehow missed the
cabins of the Hydes, the Torrances and Will Thayer in the
southern reaches of the town, and they had given up trying
to destroy John Chipman's barn. John and Gamaliel had constructed it of such stout green timber that the hurried English
and Indian pillagers were unsuccessful in burning or felling it.
The barn stood erect and trim, half buried in the thicket of
crowding poplar and sumac, the weathered sentinel of a lost
cause and a ghost community, the one structural monument
to Gamaliel's pre-war effort.

Only an awkward chimney and charred log-ends marked the spot where Painter's cabin had stood. The same ugly remnants showed where the Chandlers, the Evertses, the Bentleys and their neighbors had lived for a few uneasy seasons: a lone lilac bush, a briar-choked clearing, a rotting sledge, a heap of boulders.

At the Falls stood the shaky foundations of the Washburn sawmill which Painter had helped Chipman's father-in-law put up the year before the war. The owner had been summoned back to Connecticut to shape cannon rather than lumber, and the mill was a total loss. Most of the frame houses along Lake Champlain were gone. The forts were in shambles. The rude bridges that settlers had found time to raise were demolished, or sagged from their abutments. A mile down the road from the Painter place, the dingy log schoolhouse that had barely opened for the first classes eight years before, was in ruins. In all of the Otter Valley there was little left from the first attempts at conquering a frontier to invite resettlement—little except the land and interrupted ambition.

But the land and the ambition were enough. Hardly had the news of Yorktown been published before many of the same settlers with the same oxcarts were heading back toward the Green Mountains with larger dreams and larger equipment. They brought cattle and hogs, kettles and cribs, seeds and grafts, cherry tables and family rockers to supplement the belongings buried in the morning of war. But all the settlers did not come back; the war had taken its toll among the first families of Middlebury. There were widows, broken families and broken spirits, and a few, terrified by the memories of former trials, had forever relinquished interest in resettlement and given over their holdings to the more adventurous.

Painter had every reason to remain in Connecticut. During the war he had established connections in most of the major towns of the state. His credit was as good as his reputation. He knew the prominent craftsmen from Long Island Sound north, and they knew him. Salisbury would have been the ideal town in which to locate, for the foundries had converted it into a booming industrial center. He could easily have established himself as a cobbler or smith, a surveyor or engineer, a manufacturer or shopkeeper, but he was still devoted to the land, and he was convinced that the Vermont valleys offered better land than the Berkshire valleys. He had proved to himself and to his country that he was an able artificer, but no occupation could put to use the varied experience of an artificer like agriculture. A farmer, like an artificer, had no specialty. A good farmer had to be a builder, a blacksmith, a manufacturer, and trader, as well as tiller of soil. Moreover, he had the missionary impulse to be of service to men; in Salisbury he was not indispensable, he could be needed in a new community.

After his discharge from the Continental Army in the Spring of 1782, he spent almost a full year laying careful plans for his return to the wilderness. His finances were exhausted, but he had a canny instinct for locating resources and multiplying those resources. From a few months' miscellaneous employment he set aside enough to support his family and add to his acres in Vermont. Every shilling that he could put into land now he was sure would reap substantial dividends later.

Early in 1783 he was among the first to return to Middlebury. This time he insisted on leaving his family behind, unwilling to expose them to further frontier hardship until he had at least prepared a shelter for them, and anxious to give the boys another year of schooling. But looking speculatively into the future, one of his first moves was to add another two-hundred acre farm to the expanse of land he owned across the Creek in Cornwall. His home farm, however, was to be in Middlebury, and during the summer, with what help he could get either from newcomers or veterans at pioneering, he once more fashioned a log shelter and prepared his neglected fields for cultivation.

Assistance with heavy work was seldom a problem, for every new shelter was a community project, and any settler within reach expected to be called when he was needed. Painter himself spent as many hours laboring for others that year as he spent on his own farm. And the Hydes, the Torrances and the Thayers, as the owners of the only pre-war cabins in Middlebury, had more boarders and transients than their limited larders could afford.

By the Spring of 1784 the steady return of the settlers had developed into a migration. Scores of men, women and children were pouring into the valley, and among them came Abigail with the two boys, now husky enough to carry on a man's full fourteen-hour day of labor. There were few of the old lots on which families were not engaged in logging, house-raising, well-digging, plowing, planting or burning. The whole length of the valley echoed and resounded with the labor of many men, and the haze of smoke from the burnings hung low over them week after week. Around squalid encampments reeking of cattle, horses and offal, swarming with flies and gnats, and confused with blowing laundry, heaps of

82

household chattels, a snippy dog and bawling children, men and women worked tirelessly as if they were intent on converting a forest into a city in one season. And there were everlasting interruptions when the shout came down the valley that all hands were needed for stopping a fire that had gotten out of control, hoisting logs, or lifting a roof frame, further interruptions when the last of a side of venison had gone into the pot and the men had to take off on a hunting expedition. The turmoil in the valley was driving the game back into the mountains. Bear and deer were harder to come by, but at least there were fewer stolid bruins and nervous catamounts to menace the settlements, and even the nightly howling of the wolves and the screech of wildcats were becoming more distant.

The settlers were Painter's people. To the neglect of his own affairs, he went among them coaxing and encouraging in his blunt paternal way, as he had gone among his men during the war when their spirits were low or their prospects most appalling. This was the kind of society in which he reveled. He kept track of the progress, poking around the encampments to become acquainted, to lend a hand when he was least expected and most needed, to give a hint of practical advice without appearing over-interested. And abruptly he would disappear into the forest before his host had a chance to embarrass him with an expression of thanks. He made an appraisal of his fellow townsmen and kept quiet about it. Painter came to know them all, their family histories, their war experience, their political leanings, their capabilities and limitations: the Tuppers from Charlotte who intended to set up a tavern; Phil Ackley sawing out boards by hand for a plank house; the Sellicks; the Mungers; the Kirbys;

the Evertses' discontent with their present holdings, and the Hinmans trying to sell out to a man in Rutland.

He called on the Torrances late one afternoon and found the old veteran of the French and Indian wars molding bricks for a new residence in keeping with the demanding tastes of his wife and daughters. He stacked brick for a time and then was taken on a tour of inspection of the young orchard Torrance had started from seed before the war and had just finished grafting with cions brought up from Connecticut. He helped the old man milk his cows and measure out the milk into the tin cans that neighbors' children brought around. Torrance was as proud of his cows as he was of his daughters. He had driven the heifers up from Salisbury the previous winter in less than a week, he claimed, along with a flock of ten sheep. Painter stayed on for a scant supper of porridge and cold greens, listening for the twentieth time to Mrs. Torrance's hysterical account of how she had escaped the Indians before the war, carrying a two-year-old child on her shoulders. But the Torrances were now more fortunate than most of the neighbors; with the pre-war cabin to live in they had a head start.

The nearest neighbors of the Painters were the Chipmans, the Storys and the Smalleys. John had grandiose ideas of building a brick house in keeping with his rank of Colonel. He was broadening his fertile fields and, like Gamaliel, persuading his neighbors that a few years of labor in the valley could bring all the comforts and luxuries they had known in southern New England. The Storys and Smalleys were the only two families that had managed to weather the war in Middlebury, but neither had much to show now for their tenacity. Mrs. Story had lost her husband, and she and her children had been obliged to spend most of their time in the

84

shelter of a cave on the bank of the Otter. Mrs. Smalley had been robbed of most of her possessions, but to the end she had brazenly defied the periodic Indian intrusions.

A long list of retired Army officers were taking up residence in the vicinity. Colonel George Sloan had bought the Slasson pitch and was carrying on from where Eleazer left off. Though Slasson had built one of the first cabins before the war and fathered the first child born in the town, he and his wife had found the climate too rigorous and the Vermont wilderness too remote for their tastes. Sam Bentley had reached the same conclusion and sold out his pitch to Benjamin Risley. But Captain Stephen Goodrich, new arrival from Glastonbury, Connecticut, with his two sons Amos and William, had enough spirit to make up for any deficiency of other war-wearied veterans.

Biggest landowner in the neighborhood was Daniel Foot, an incorrigible pioneer who, at the age of sixty, after converting two Massachusetts wilderness areas into productive farms, was now setting out to conquer a thousand Middlebury acres. "He could never be contented with a well-cultivated farm," claimed one of his critics. "There must be forests to subdue, or it is no place for him." Five grown sons and a married daughter were of the same cut, and all were occupied in 1784 with separate agricultural enterprises on neighboring pitches, while circulating prejudiced propaganda that they were building the future business center of Middlebury. Painter had enemies as well as friends in the community, and Daniel Foot was one of them: "a high tempered, boastful man, conceited, vulgar and highly inelegant in ye house." It would take time to teach Daniel that the center would be in the southern end of town.

Despite the presence of womenfolk, it was a man's frontier

85

society in which Gamaliel moved. They were all farmers, the women as well as the men, and frequently there was little differentiating in the labor of the two. A woman was usually found at the other end of a crosscut saw; she did the milking if the family owned a cow. She tended the sheep and tethered the horses when she was not occupied with her children. She was given the lighter work of harrowing the corn with the oxen while the men were logging, or stripping bark for roofing and flooring while the men were hauling stone.

Painter's farm-minded neighbors were scrupulous in their own way, some of them a little rowdy, few with any conspicuous refinement, men and women with prodigious appetites for hard work, mean fare, and backwoods discomfort. As newcomers arrived, he and Abigail were ready to put them up for a night, offer them a modest meal, assist them in salvaging rusted kettles and warped furniture from the caches they had made before leaving, or help them locate the farm site they had purchased while in Connecticut and never seen. And he had laconic counsel for detached adventurers like the young Long Islander, John Tillotson, who arrived penniless in the summer of 1784 and was promptly referred to the Chandlers who had an eligible and eager daughter. Or his loft was ready for the entertainment of transient pastors like Nathan Perkins who wrote unappreciatively of what he found in the environment. "Log huts—people nasty—poor—low-lived —indelicate—and miserable cooks. All sadly parsimonious— many profane—yet cheerful and much more contented than in Hartford—and the women more contented than ye men— turned tawny by ye smoke of ye log huts—dress coarse, and mean, & nasty, & ragged.—Some very clever women and men —serious and sensible. Scarcely any politeness . . . —all work,

86

& yet ye women quiet,—serene,—peaceable,—contented, loving their husbands, their home,—wanting never to return,—nor any dressy clothes; . . . tough are they, brawny their limbs, —their young girls unpolished—& will bear work as well as mules. Woods make people love one another & kind and obliging and good natured. They set much more by one another than in ye old settlements. Leave their doors unbarred. Sleep quietly amid flees—bed buggs—dirt & rags."

Painter saw the drudgery and squalor in the community he was fathering, but he saw little that was vulgar among the families he knew better than Perkins, families with their grown sons and daughters, a few bachelor-hermits, war widows with their small children, families eager to preserve their Bay State religion while struggling with the Vermont laws of nature. He saw an Arcadian life, a community in which all were on the same social level, all on the same economic level. There was usually an adequacy of the simpler necessities, and what one family lacked could be readily borrowed from another, or in a few days procured from a trading post at Ticonderoga or Rutland. Hope and enthusiasm made them blind to the squalor and insensible to the drudgery.

Middlebury was a community both in purpose and spirit. No man labored alone. As the harvests ripened, whole families moved from one field to the next, the men working from morning to night with scythes, cradles, rakes and forks, the women pooling their provisions for a common feast. A summer work day of fifteen to eighteen hours was commonplace, and Painter seemed to find more hours in the day than anyone else. Despite his circumambulation, his fields of barley and wheat were as well-kept as another's, his corn as amply cultivated, his fences as stout and high, his wife and children as well cared for. As a farmer he was as obdurate as any of his weeds, as resourceful as the black squirrels and deer that preyed on his acres. Where the forest was still uncut, he envisioned his corn stretching out acre after acre, a larger flax field near the creek, row on row of field beans and field peas. He would try rye and oats among the stumps another year, and hope for a better yield of potatoes. Abigail would have more cleared ground for her garden of cabbage and onions, beets, carrots, cucumbers, melons and squashes. And not to be outdone by old Torrance, in time he would have an apple and pear orchard with Durham sweetings, Roxbury russets, Spitzenburgs and Seek-no-furthers; he would transplant some of the native plum trees into his backyard, high bush cranberries, currant bushes, gooseberries and raspberries; Eleazar Claghorn had promised him a few clippings from his grapevine, and along the fence where hop vines were stretching up he had started a row of black cherry seedlings. A good hive of bees had been captured, and with luck he could count on thirty or forty pounds of honey, come October. The stand of maples to the north should give him an adequate supply of sugar next spring.

It would take a long time, but the Painter farm would be the envy of the Valley. Abigail was already working on the flax, a tedious job. It had to be plucked, dried, threshed, steeped, dried again, beaten, hung, bruised, and then patiently carded and combed before it would be ready for spinning and weaving. Abigail had the patience to see the whole process through to the finish, and by Christmas she would be stitching him a shirt grown from his own rich loam.

Next year he would have sheep to shear and more work for Abigail. To her would fall the task of washing the fleece,

88

combing out the burrs and briars, spinning the yarn, carding it for cloth, fulling the wool under water, drying, knitting and weaving it.

It was all part of the life of farming—wool-raising, flax-growing, dairying, crop cultivation, building and brewing. Only those subsisting in the last throes of poverty stooped to drinking water as a table beverage. Rum was available, and as essential to the diet as sweetening or salt, but one usually had to pay cash for it, and there was little cash. The Painters hadn't descended to drinking water, and they would have beer as soon as his barley was harvested and the brew given time to work. Preparing the barley would be a long smelly job, the steeping, sprouting, drying and crushing into malt, the brewing, mashing, drawing off, mixing with hops, fermenting and bunging. But it was no less tedious and no less gratifying than all the other farmstead industry: curing cheese; smoking meat; making soap and tallow; joining; tanning; shodding and chopping. Abigail had the zest to do a man's work, and with Samuel and Joseph now equal to almost any task on the farm, the family could be economically self-sufficient in another season or two.

Gamaliel was not given to expression of happiness, but never in his life had he been more contented; never had the future looked more secure or more promising. The war had been worth fighting. The dreams he had shaped during the dull hours at Fishkill and at Tottawa were materializing. He had good neighbors, decent shelter, a healthy family and the start of a farm that would have brought envy from any of his artificer friends in Connecticut. He thanked God in his own prayers and in the faltering family prayers around the rough hewn table of his log cabin.

And it all came to an end in one day when a crew of burly surveyors were seen tramping across his fields with their lines and instruments. They represented the Surveyor General, he was informed brusquely. They were correcting the town boundaries, and as they made slashes on his trees behind the house, they told him he was nothing but a squatter. The land he had cleared and planted was not his land. He had pitched in Salisbury, not Middlebury. His house was in Salisbury on land that belonged to someone else. His clearing was in Salisbury. All but thirty of the two hundred acres he had fenced off were on the wrong side of the line. He protested their insults, argued, and tried to reason. He explained something of what the land meant to him and begged for understanding. They understood, but they were not paid to pity. He convinced them that he was a surveyor, too, and asked to see the evidence. Proudly the maps were displayed, and at once the facts were as indisputable as they were incredible. He read their charts and knew the truth. Painter, the accomplished surveyor, had suddenly become the subject of a grim penalty for another surveyor's error made nearly a quarter of a century before, when Middlebury was being marked out of the wilderness by speculators in towns rather than farms. John Everts in his haste to stake off an ample area had miscalculated gravely. Both the north and the south lines of the town were misplaced. Not a modest error of a few yards, but a generous blunder of forty rods. And Painter, after all his trials, toil and patience, was facing ignominious ruin. The corn, the barley, the flax and the cabin were no longer legally his. His dreams and his work for over a decade had been exploded in futility. He would have to begin all over again. The Salisbury town line was officially moved north by the autocratic Surveyor General, and over a scribbled signature the Painters were eliminated as residents of the town he had been fathering.

The proprietors of Salisbury would readily have granted him residence and the purchase right of a two-hundred acre pitch in that town. Or he could have moved across the Creek to his estate in Cornwall where he would have been welcomed as a leading citizen. But Painter was a part of Middlebury. His exertions had been spent on the establishment of a community called Middlebury; he was devoted to it; his ambitions and sentiment were for Middlebury. He spurned bids to settle in any other town even when Salisbury magnanimously elected him its representative to the Assembly.

No one tried to oust him from the land. No one would have had the courage or the cruelty to attempt it. The citizens of Middlebury would have joined the citizens of Salisbury in rising to his defense. But in his own mind it was humiliatingly clear that he was a squatter. Still he made no move to leave during the winter or the following spring. He planted his corn again, but there was no expanding of the clearing as he had planned. He did not set out an orchard. He had experienced bitter adversity before, but nothing that cut him like this. His Middlebury friends assured him that at the next town meeting he would be granted the privilege of taking his pick of any unassigned lot in the town. Gamaliel reckoned that he was entitled to such consideration, but the choicest farm land was already spoken for. He was still young in years, but suddenly he felt too old in spirit to begin clearing another two hundred acres, going through the process of ringing trees, burning, cutting, stumping, the struggle to keep down brush and let in light. He stayed on in Salisbury, and some of the brush crept back into the sides of his clearing.

Disconsolately he went back to surveying. Settlers in all the surrounding towns were clamoring for his services. While his own farm and family suffered neglect, he measured off scores of lots for others. And one evening on his return he paused at the Falls where he had helped Chipman's father-in-law put up a sawmill before the war and where Washburn was again laying foundations for a new mill. Perhaps indeed Washburn had the right idea; Gamaliel himself had seen it in his war-time tours of duty in southern New England, in New York and New Jersey: the center of a town invariably was the mill. First a sawmill, then a gristmill, woolen mills later on. All roads led to a waterfall. His home should be at the center, and here was land that no one claimed, land that no farmer wanted, for good reasons. It was ledge and clay which offered scant footing even for the hemlock forest that covered the slopes. Clear away the tangle of uprooted trees, rotting trunks and prickly ash, and grain would not grow here, but industry might. Painter struggled over the fallen logs and pushed his way through the forest to the foot of the Falls where a mass of dead trees constantly swirled in the eddy. The revolving of those tons of logs, Painter thought, was a good example of the power in that water roaring over the fifty-foot drop. Washburn's mill foundation above looked strangely precarious on the edge of the tide.

Fatigued though he was from the long day of tramping, he scaled the sheer cliff alongside the fall, deafened by the roar and thoroughly dampened by the blown spray. He followed the rough woods path Washburn had cut to the top of the rise a hundred yards above the Creek, and on the brow of the hill paced off acres with a practiced stride. Facing west into the sunset through a break in the trees he could make out the hazy line of the Adirondacks; to the east the stark line of the Green Mountains. He visualized the area stripped of its trees and wondered why none had bothered to consider it as a home site—or a town site. It was the wildest spot in the whole town, but it could be the most important. The only persons living in the region were Asa Blodgett and "Hop" Johnson. Asa kept a simple log hut for creek travelers on the Cornwall side, and Hop a similar establishment on the Middlebury side. Both stocked a good supply of poor liquor which they sold cheaply to their undistinguished clientele, and "Hop," when he felt inclined, ran a ferry for foot passengers. Surely neither of them had any other occupational interest in the area. It was mighty poor farm land, but sooner or later, Painter assured himself, this rugged ground was bound to be the focal point of the community. Then and there he decided to gamble on a new pitch.

At the April town meeting in 1785, the Surveyor General's dislocation of the town line was on the agenda for warm dispute. The new bounds were final, but before the meeting was adjourned, Painter was granted "the privilege of re-pitching land in lieu of what was cut off by said line." To replace the 170 acres he had lost, he chose fifty—"the Mill lot" that embraced the whole of the east side of the falls: "beginning at a cherry tree, which stands forty links to a stake near a red ash tree marked, which is the southwest corner of a two hundred acre pitch laid out to Joshua Hyde . . . thence east on the south line of said pitch 26 chains and 50 links to a maple staddle, thence south 34 chains and

30 links to a hemlock tree, thence west 12 chains and 75 links to an elm staddle standing on the bank of Otter Creek, thence following down the creek as it runs to the bound begun at." Most of the future center of the village of Middlebury belonged to him.

For two more years Painter and his family lived on in Salisbury on the land that did not belong to them. But his interest was no longer in the farm. He grubbed a good subsistence from it, but he cleared no more stumps, and the young shoots that sprang up ravenously around the old stumps remained untrimmed. The size of his fields shrank, and the length of his rows shortened. He was busy at the Falls helping his father-in-law complete the sawmill. Washburn's interests were now his interests, and the old man in his middle sixties needed Gamaliel's help. Already the settlers who wanted to replace their log huts with frame houses were floating logs down the Creek and accumulating piles to be squared for beams and joists.

Daniel Foot, noting a good thing in what Painter and Washburn were doing, and not wanting to be outdone by anyone, procured the land and water rights on the Cornwall side of the Falls and started putting up a similar structure across the Creek, not a hundred feet away. Painter could hardly hope for anything better. There was enough lumber and enough demand for six mills. He kept his ideas on creating a town center to himself and continued to disagree with Foot on practically everything except mill construction. Foot had his gang of sons working for him and made even more rapid progress than Painter and Washburn. It was nip and tuck competition, and before winter set in both mills were turning out lumber, whining at each other above the

94

roar of the falls. Then as a final gesture to prove to himself that he was giving up farming for good, Painter sold two hundred acres of his land in Cornwall and put away the seventy-five pounds to invest in Middlebury industry. As every frontiersman was a farmer of sorts, he would always be a farmer; he would set out his orchard at the Falls; he would have horses, cows, and a broad garden, but it would never again be his major occupation.

5 SHERIFF

In 1785 Addison County was a great, sprawling area, extending all the way from the Middlebury-Salisbury area on the south, to the Canadian Border on the north, and from Lake Champlain eastward well over the crest of the Green Mountains, some four thousand sparsely settled square miles. Yet even this vast area was minuscule in comparison with the dimensions of counties to which it had belonged. Already it had been weaned five times. For nearly a century the Addison area was part of Albany County, which included all of Vermont and a lion's share of Massachusetts. In 1772, it became a segment of Charlotte, comprising all of western Vermont; and when Charlotte was overthrown six years later, everything

97

east of the mountain became the County of Unity; everything west, Bennington. But jealous patriots resented nominal attachment of the better half of Vermont to the unpopular Benning, and at the height of the Revolution the County grabbed the name of the American hero of the hour, George Washington. However, the connection was short-lived. By the time a map came from the printers, Washington had lost out in favor of Rutland, and in Rutland County Middlebury remained until October 18, 1785, when the huge northern half was divorced and Addison became an entity.

As evidence that the unkempt settlers were not entirely bereft of literary leanings, or carried away with political prejudice, the new county, as well as the town, was named for a Britisher, the author of the Sir Roger de Coverly Papers. What the affinity was between Joseph Addison and the American Addisonians is lost in the confusion of chronicles. Certainly the suave ghost of Addison would have reared in protest at any comparison between his convictions and theirs. Some founder of the Town of Addison may have remembered a kinship with the journalist and elected to do him honor, or the original proprietors may have jumped to the conclusion that the poet was a kinspirit after discovering a few sympathetic lines that gave voice to their sentiments:

A day, an hour, of virtuous liberty
Is worth a whole eternity of bondage.

In any case, the spacious County became the namesake of the man who glorified spaciousness, "with all the blue eternal sky." Addison County had some 3500 square miles of it, seventy-five miles in length by fifty across, and in 1785 it began its corporate existence with a clerk, judge, side judges, sheriff, high bailiff, states attorney and the power to establish the machinery of civil government. To Gamaliel Painter went the appointment of side judge, and as such it would have been his privilege to mete out justice to his fellow men, sitting in state at Judge Strong's dining room table in Addison, on the first Tuesday of March and at Captain Butterfield's more modest kitchen table in Colchester on the second Tuesday of November.

But Gamaliel's modesty was commensurate with his ignorance of law. He was not convinced that the dignity of judgeship was entirely becoming. If he were to be a public servant, his preference was to serve outdoors. He knew the lay of the County land better than he knew the lay of County jurisprudence. The job of sheriff was open for 1786, and with a third of Vermont to cover, there would be much more adventure in active law enforcement than in producing ponderous judgements. After sitting with the opening session of the Court, he respectfully turned in his resignation, and gave up the gavel for the privilege of wearing the badge.

A sheriff was endowed with almost autocratic authority in this frontier society. He was the Law. It was his duty to "conserve the peace, and to suppress, with force and strong hand, when the necessity of the case shall so require, all tumults, riots, routs, and other unlawful assemblies; and to apprehend, without warrant, all such as he shall find so as aforesaid appearing in the disturbance of the peace." He could round up every able-bodied male in the County to assist in the execution of his duty as he saw it, and "whosoever being of age and ability, and being so commanded, shall neglect or refuse to yield his assistance to any sheriff . . . shall pay a fine of twelve pounds." He had power to call out the militia, and all military officers and soldiers were "commanded to yield obedience to the sheriff's commands." With a warrant in his possession, he had authority to search houses "in matters of delinquency or of a criminal nature", and any man who refused him entrance or abused him in any way was subject to a fine of a hundred pounds. He had to be sworn in personally by the Governor, bonded for two thousand pounds, and on the eve of court sessions range over the county with his deputies, serving writs and escorting unwilling culprits and witnesses to the seat of justice. It was far more uncompromising to one's prospective political stature to take on an unpleasant job of the people, involving direct contact with the people, than to set oneself on the pedestal of a judgeship.

But Painter was inclined to confuse delegated duties with his own interpretation of public welfare and even his personal ambitions. He was not above using his position as Sheriff to promote his interest in creating a village at Middlebury Falls. Legally he was somewhat justified, for State Statutes required every town to designate its center and "most public place", if for no other reason than to set up its stocks. Punishment of offenders had to be executed in the most public place, and Middlebury had no most public place. The townspeople all had acquired an unshakable conviction that the center should be established within a few hundred yards of their several front doors, and could not settle their differences sufficiently even to decide on a spot where the lawbreakers could be publicly aired.

It took a stubborn hand like the new Sheriff's to bring some kind of order out of the chaos of discord. He had a professional interest in having the stocks available for use, and he had a personal interest in seeing that they were set up at the Falls. Since people could not agree with one another, he could use the strong arm to encourage their agreement with him. "Each town in this State," he quoted from the Statutes, "shall maintain and, as often as the same shall be necessary, make at their own charge, a good pair of stocks, with a lock and key sufficient to secure offenders who shall be sentenced to sit therein; *which stocks shall be erected in the most public place in each respective town.*"

Painter had a point—not a very reliable one—but it was serviceable, and he made the most of it. In the name of the law he demanded that stocks be set up at the Falls. And he proceeded to buttress his demand with plans to create a trading and industrial center in full view of the stocks.

During the Spring of 1786 catastrophe at the Falls momentarily appeared to thwart his plan. The sawmill which he had helped Washburn put through to completion before snow fell the previous winter was constructed with gross lack of foresight. It encroached dangerously on the right of way of Otter Creek and was inadequately shanked to withstand what a rebellious March could do to man's invention. One spring thaw did its worst. Snow went off and ice went out together that year, accompanied by heavy rains. The Creek poured over its banks and thundered over the falls, carrying jams of ice with it. The mill was awash; it took the buffeting for a few hours, and then with a rumble hardly audible above the roar and crunch of ice going over the falls, slid down the embankment, leaving scarcely a trace of where it had been. Foot's mill on the opposite Cornwall bank stood firm and defiant against the onslaught.

It was the second mill that Washburn had lost, and he decided to go back to farming. But Painter, with his usual genius for turning adversity to good account, whether the adversity was his own or another's, suavely made arrangements to take over all of Washburn's holdings adjacent to his own. He secured the land; he secured the water rights. He doubled his stake in the future site of the village and determined to create a mill where he could easily keep an eye on the stocks. A miller's was a good secondary occupation for a sheriff. To reassure himself that he had total faith in Middlebury, as well as to provide capital for his project, he broke the last economic tie connecting him to his native state, and disposed of the modest tract of land his father had left him in Connecticut. The washout at the Falls and the elevation to the position of sheriff had convinced him with finality that he should make a career of making Middlebury.

Every able-bodied mason, carpenter and drayman who could be induced to leave a harrow, a cornfield, or a timber lot, was put to work at good wages on a sawmill that was to overshadow Foot's and make Washburn's attempt look like a lean-to. He avoided all the errors Washburn had discovered the hard way. Painter's sawmill was built on solid rock at the head of the falls, well back from the high-water mark. Its foundations were heavy limestone, held together with the best mortar. The walls and roof were of stout, sided timber from his newly acquired acres. It was not a pretty structure, but it would take more than the wrath of the Otter to destroy it. All the talents of the artificer went into the structure. He built with the speed and the solidity he had learned in the experience of his Revolutionary years. Before the end of the season it was in operation, and further foundations were being laid for a gristmill which would compete with any services that Foot might render on the opposite side of the Creek.

What Painter needed most was a lieutenant, a reliable boss carpenter to handle the construction work while he was fulfilling his professional obligations as sheriff or pursuing some of his other multiple interests. He looked covetously across the Creek at Foot's right-hand man, a partially domesticated tramp named Simeon Dudley, who had lived for several years in a Cornwall shanty and proven his worth in most of the Foot construction jobs as a rough-and-ready artisan. The Sheriff needed Dudley. He talked propositions with Foot and got nowhere. He talked with Dudley's friends and found them too loyal to their own camp to portray interest in his. Finally he talked to Dudley. It was the Painter persuasion, the wage scale, the badge, and probably a little liquor that won Simeon. After cultivating an argument with Foot, Dudley forded the stream under cover of darkness, set up a chimneyless hut for himself, and went to work for Painter. The miller went off to attend his neglected duties as Sheriff.

His friend Ethan Allen, long back from British imprisonment, was on the rampage again, this time exhausting his spleen on a neighbor, Rufus Perigo, whom he accused of trespass and misappropriation of property. Painter had to summon Perigo to the seat of justice "holden at Captain Thomas Butterfield's in Colchester," and there, standing guard over the accused, he learned of the extent of the pillage Perigo had committed. According to Ethan, the offender had been forcibly and unlawfully cutting, carrying off and destroying on the land, tenements and possessions of the plaintiff in Burlington, oak, pine, and other valuable timber and . . . 100 sticks of white oak and square timber to the damage of the plaintiff 100 pounds." According to the accused, he had merely been clearing his own land. Both Ethan and Ira Allen had claimed possession of thousands of acres of land in the Winooski Valley. They had become unduly sensitive to the encroachment of men not to their liking, and made themselves thoroughly unpopular with their threats and intimidations. Like most of their other disputes, Ethan lost this one, and Sheriff Painter had no small satisfaction in releasing Perigo.

But at the same session in another case of trespass and alleged theft, Painter saw the defendant assessed over twenty-one pounds and damages for making off with "one good iron-shod sleigh and harness and one horse, all the said sleigh, harness and horse to be well worth £20."

There were humor, pathos, and bitterness in these backwoods trials which Painter in his official capacity had to accept without expression of interest, compassion, or concern, though he felt a definite sympathy for Alexander Campbell, who was suing Nathaniel Soumi for "unjustly detaining 3 hogsheads of rum, 1 box of Tea, 7 pieces of woolen cloth, 9 pieces of linen, and a number of dry cod fish." Campbell wanted to collect a thousand pounds for his loss. He got five pounds, seventeen shillings and twopence.

And when Sheriff Painter brought in Silas Holbrook to stand before a blind plaintiff, Mary Jones, he wished that he might have settled with the defendant without benefit of trial. Mary had been afflicted with a painful tumor on her eyelid and in desperation had accepted the services of "Doctor" Holbrook, a self-appointed physician. "The said defendant in the capacity of a physician undertook to extirpate and heal the same . . . though the defendant had no knowledge in extirpating and healing said wen or tumor and he made and directed such application as was improper for extirpating said wen, but was very hurtful, and wholly coroded her eyelid which has fell off and also lost the use of her eye." Mary and her husband were suing for damages of a hundred pounds. The bench was convinced of Holbrook's culpability, but Painter was as dissatisfied as the Joneses with the settlement imposed by Judge Strong, fifteen pounds instead of a hundred.

There were other court decisions dealing with tavern keepers, deeds, debts, and desertions. And as Painter witnessed judgment in the making from the vantage point of the Sheriff's stand, he gradually lost some of the misgivings about his own ability to serve on the bench. On the forty-mile trip back to Middlebury, he convinced himself that the position of judge had almost as many merits as the office of Sheriff.

Due perhaps to the respect in which Sheriff Painter was held in his home territory, due, more likely, to the fact that his neighbors were too preoccupied with personal troubles to create community trouble, he had little law enforcement to consume his time at the southern end of the County. There were no riots to quell, no tumults to settle, no routs to contend with, in fact, little of the excitement that the law made provision for him to oppose.

At the Falls, major events were occurring in addition to his own building projects. Simeon Dudley had carelessly let his shack burn down one evening while under the influence, and Daniel Foot had started preparations for constructing a bridge. The loss of Simeon's hovel was no catastrophe; he could put up another in a matter of hours, but Painter was anxious to see a little more style to any kind of new residence erected in the vicinity. He offered him counsel on a more appropriate standard of living, gave the boss carpenter time off from the mill, helped him draw up plans for a substantial frame house, and set him to work. Meantime, Painter came to terms with Daniel Foot and occasionally lent his Cornwall competitor a hand and a few engineering principles on the proper laying of a log bridge.

The Foots couldn't have engaged themselves in a project more to his liking if he had ordered it. Actually, the Sheriff, doubling as a Representative from Salisbury, had done his best to order it by proposing to the Legislature a bill "for levying a tax of twopence on each acre of land in the towns of Middlebury and Salisbury, in Addison county, for making and repairing roads and bridges." The impartial delegates, however, detecting a proposition that would benefit Middlebury more than Salisbury, declined their support until Painter had changed the bill to apply only to Middlebury. But funds made available by the act could scarcely provide a start on all the public works needed in the town. Roads and bridges were called for in every quarter, and in the end it was decided that the treasury could not be emptied for the benefit of the few who espoused the cause of bridge making at the Falls. With the tacit approval of the town freemen, and promises of contributions in labor from supporters, the Foots took on the project, connecting their lumber yard with one Painter was laying out on the opposite side.

There may have been a scheme behind Foot's charity in providing this link between Cornwall and Middlebury, but scheme or charity, the bridge even with toll could be more useful to Painter than to Foot. It could draw trade to the

Foot establishment, but it would also bring trade to him. Painter willingly contributed his own time and his men to the effort. Logs were laid as abutments, jutting out as they rose, leaving a span of some seventy feet. Some of the enormous pine logs which had been withheld from King George's navy formed single string-pieces across this span, and the trestle was then floored with poles. Despite its deficiencies in appearance and stability, the bridge became the first wonder of the County. Men came miles to see it, and children, out of sight of their elders, found supreme delight in bouncing on the center, or sitting on the edge with legs over the side watching the turbulence of water sweeping over the falls. The bridge was safe enough for any ordinary team of horses or pair of oxen, for any ordinary conveyance and the load, but it had more pliability than suited a squeamish transient. It was narrow, the sides were open, and the white rapids a few feet below brought terror to anyone lacking full confidence in the handiwork of Daniel Foot and Gamaliel Painter.

At once all roads turned toward the bridge. The muddy slough from the Lake bent toward it; the ruts from Cornwall led there with purpose; and the trail on the east side of the Creek from Vergennes made a detour in its direction. The mills and the bridge had turned the traffic as Painter had intended.

Demands on the miller and sheriff for participation in public affairs were constant. Despite his being a squatter in Salisbury, the town insisted on electing him as their first Assembly representative, and Middlebury, which had no representative, was urging him to stand as their candidate. As a justice of the peace he was called upon to witness and affirm land transfers in a period when such transfers were a daily occurrence. The

Assembly elected him first Surveyor for Addison County. He was appointed by Salisbury to lay out the roads in that town, and elected by Cornwall to divide the town into church societies by way of settling a stalemate over the most suitable location for churches. People wanting land surveys gave him no peace; during the summer of 1786, in Middlebury alone he recorded no less than fifteen such surveys, and surrounding towns placed equal demands on his services. He had a bewildering series of roles as Sheriff, moderator, surveyor, miller, justice of peace, and peacemaker, and Ira Allen was trying to get him to invest in a huge real estate venture in the Winooski Valley, but his major interest was still in creating a village as a trading and industrial center, not only for the town of Middlebury, but also for surrounding towns which lacked the ideal location he had chosen.

Before he had completed his year as Sheriff, once more he was urged to add the office of Judge to all his other titles. It was too tempting to turn down now, but his resignation as Sheriff left county law enforcement in such a predicament that the State Legislature had to pass a special bill to cope with the situation:

> Whereas the late Sheriff of the County of Addison, at the beginning of this session resigned his said office; by means whereof services of writs and executions made by his deputies, may be void in law, and many inconveniences may arise thereon; therefore Be it enacted by the General Assembly of the State of Vermont, that the service of all writs and other acts done by the Deputy Sheriffs in the County of Addison, in the execution of their office, since the resignation of the said Sheriff, and before the fifth day of November, next, shall be as good and effectual in law, as if the said Sheriff had not resigned his said office: any law to the contrary notwithstanding.

108

A Sheriff could live in a log cabin, but a Judge was expected to have a less commonplace residence. It was time for him to move to the Falls where his gristmill was nearing completion. He eyed the house that he had persuaded Simeon Dudley to build; it was shaping up better than he had supposed. He considered the long commuting distance to his cabin in Salisbury, talked it over with Abigail, and finally drew a bargain. Painter moved into the new frame house, rather than Simeon Dudley.

He had given up farming, the military, the informality of serving as sheriff, and had competent help to operate his mill. He was at last settled in his first frame house and could look forward to a life of respectability. From his windows there was little he could see which as yet hinted of civilization, but his imagination could easily clear the forest which hemmed in his home site, and put in its place a row of trading posts, more homes like his own, a few village streets and public buildings, a tavern with a stagecoach stop, and even a postal station to take the place of the nearest one now offering the settlers service in Rutland. Other people still had convictions about locating the town center several miles to the south and to the east, but with a bridge, the mills, a cluster of homes on the Cornwall side, and his own house at the Falls, Painter knew he had a head start. From now on it would be a problem of propaganda in getting people accustomed to coming to the Falls and thinking of the Falls as their rendezvous.

To initiate the campaign, Gamaliel and Abigail opened Middlebury's social season for the winter of 1787 on Christmas day with a housewarming such as few of the settlers had seen in Connecticut, Massachusetts or Vermont since before the War. The whole town, as well as representatives from neighboring towns, were invited; they all came—on ox-drawn sleds, in wagons, on foot, and they put aside their differences on the location of a village green long enough to josh Gamaliel for locating in such a remote quarter. He accepted the quips in good spirit and without attempt to convert anyone to his conviction. Instead he offered another helping of veni· son, another mug of hot rum or another scoop of Indian pudding.

His carpenter, Simeon Dudley, was as much an honored guest as Colonel Sumner who had settled two miles north the previous summer. The whole family of Foots, Daniel, Freeman, Stillman, and John, were there out of curiosity and envy. Colonel Seth Storrs rode in from Addison. The Chipman families were there. "Hop" Johnson and his brood strolled over from the "tavern" with a gift of brandy. The Washburns, the Goodriches, Mr. and Mrs. Tillotson, new families like the Wadsworths, the Mungers, and the Prestons, all came to pay their respects and join in the fun. The party overflowed the house and spread out to the packed snow in the yard. They visited the sawmill, ambled over the bridge, played cops and robbers in the hemlock forest. By nightfall the men were well fortified and the women were segregated in the kitchen end of the house. What little space was available became a dance floor. Fathers went home to do the chores, and the young folk stayed on into the night. Samuel Bartholomew, the county poet, after sobering the next day, summarized the spirit of the party in eight lines:

> This place called Middlebury Falls
> Is like a castle without walls.
> Surrounded 'tis by hemlock trees

SHERIFF

> Which shut out all its enemies.
> The pow-wow now on Christmas day,
> Which much resembled Indian play,
> I think will never be forgotten
> Till all the hemlock trees are rotten.

The townsfolk did not know it at the time, but they had been sold a bill of goods. The Falls had begun to come into its own.

6 JUDGE

Locally in the New England back country, Court and Church worked hand in hand to suppress vice, temper iniquity, and dissipate the frailties of the flesh, but even with this close institutional association, frequently there was more law than order. Where either Court or Church was derelict, transgression flourished, licentiousness reigned.

For more than two decades after the War, the moral and spiritual welfare of Middlebury was in a precarious state; there was an efficient, though transient, Court, but there was no Church. For any community with pretentions to righteousness it was a deplorable deficiency. Respectful of the Almighty as were the citizens of Middlebury, they had no regard for each other's opinion on where He should be worshipped. The settlements were spread across an area of over twenty thousand acres, and with no family of respectability ready to cross many more acres than his own to attend Meeting, the Court had a double responsibility for enforcement of the laws of God and man, and that responsibility fell largely upon Judge Painter.

Painter, representing the Court, had "cognizance of all criminal matters of every name and nature", "original jurisdiction" over all civil actions, and since there was little distinguishing between crime and sin or between civil and ecclesiastical authority, the Judge was as much concerned with the laws of Moses as the laws of Vermont. He was required to have at least one other judge present to constitute a court, and alone had authority only to open or adjourn a session, but his major duties as side judge were to rove about the town and county offering private reproof to backsliders, warning and counsel to those subject to temptation, a chief inquisitor gathering intelligence that might prove of value in a day of judgment. He was expected to serve as a model of decency, worthy of the respect and deference of his clientele. That his judicial services were most effective in the immediate vicinity of Middlebury was evident from the fact that the sorriest cases which came to the official attention of his Court were beyond the immediate limits of the town.

But Painter, more than any other, realized his own inadequacies in attempting to combine the preoccupation of pastor with the occupation of Judge. Middlebury needed a qualified pastor to help quell the free spirit of the settlers; it needed a church organization, and an edifice to symbolize the existence of that organization. But all this depended on a decision

114

as to where the pastor would preach and where the church would be built. Painter knew that the only logical location was at the Falls, but work as hard as he might, indoors and out, with persuasion, contrivance and threat, he could not rally the community to agreement. At the very first business meeting of the town in 1788, the principal item on the agenda was "to choose a committee to stick a stake for the meeting house." The Committee was appointed. It met, wrangled, and disagreed. Other committees took its place with the same result, and when the members of one committee could reach approximate agreement, the town set itself against them. Time and again the temperature of the argument over where the stake should be stuck rose to the combustion point. And Judge Painter was so outspoken in his resolve to locate the meetinghouse at the Falls, he was given little opportunity to serve on committees chosen to break the deadlock. His prejudices were all too well known. In his capacity as Judge he contrived to carry much of the burden that should have been carried by a pastor.

When services were held, Painter was obliged to swallow his pride and listen to John Chipman's gritty rendition of the scriptures in Daniel Foot's barn. Daniel's barn was the biggest, the best, and the emptiest, and the owner took more than civic pride in being able to draw the populace to his property in the eastern part of the town where he and members of his family owned several farms. It was an insufferable indignity to the Judge to have to accept communal hospitality there, but until a better building was available there was no choice. Every kind of public gathering was held there, and on one occasion Painter was even obliged to conduct a hearing at Foot's when no other than the owner of the barn was the defendant. Daniel had been accused of obstructing a highway, and the evidence against him was clear. In fact, Gamaliel had proven him guilty in a justice's writ and levied the fine, whereupon a special town meeting was called to rebuke the Judge and negate the prosecution. Daniel packed the meeting with his friends and had the effrontery to move that the fine, being the property of the town, be relinquished and "directions given the Selectmen not to collect the fine." To the Judge's utter humiliation, the motion was seconded, and "the vote being put was carried in the affirmative."

Painter was adequate to any minor argument out of doors, but words failed him when he faced major opposition in the formality of a town meeting. He could never think of the proper retort until afterwards; when an occasion demanded eloquence he lost his tongue. Supported by other judges in court he was relatively at ease, but his real forte was in scouring the countryside for evidence of iniquity, tracing down rumors of scandal, and settling the case before the evidence or the rumors reached the ears of official Justice.

His territory was only a fraction of what it had been when he was sheriff, for in 1787, just before he assumed the office of Judge, the Assembly carved up Addison County for the last time. The bill was passed by a narrow margin, and Painter's vote in favor of the division helped to carry the issue. The northern half was re-named Chittenden, and Addison was restricted to a modest area reaching from Lake Champlain to the eastern slopes of the Green Mountain range, and from Lake Dunmore north beyond Monkton Pond. Vermont was now composed of six counties, most of which were still to suffer considerable dismemberment, but Addison, except for a few minor contractions and expansions, was fixed, and the jurisdiction of the Court accordingly covered only the southern fringe of its former arena. Painter made no more judicial excursions to Colchester, five miles north of Burlington.

The County had a well organized Court, meeting regularly twice a year in March and November at a variety of private homes and public houses; it still had no courthouse, and when it did get one, Painter had convinced himself and his friends that it should not be located in Addison where courts had legally been authorized to meet. The geographical center of the County was much nearer Middlebury. He had the ideal spot for it on the slope next to his house; as representative in the Assembly he was in a fair position to put over the proposition of locating it there and converting Middlebury into the shire town. And not above a little duplicity, the thought crossed his mind that a courthouse located at the Falls would make a more inviting edifice for the accommodation of a church than Daniel Foot's barn.

Unceremoniously he deeded to the County a plot of land north of his house, and one day announced to an unsuspecting group of first citizens to whom he was playing host, "This is the place for the Courthouse." They were standing just outside his north fence, waist high in underbrush and surrounded by a confusion of felled trees and decaying stumps. His listeners nodded their condescension, smiled inwardly at his conceit, and refrained from making any commitment of approval. It was a matter that time and the Judge could settle, but not one of them could immediately think of a more desirable site; besides they were more interested in where a village church would be placed than in the location of the County courthouse. Painter detected their indifference and proceeded to take advantage of it. He could afford to expend patience on an issue as important as this. Behind scenes he went to work.

Meantime he attended court sessions at Captain Zadock Everet's, at Jonah Case's, in Sam Mattock's public house, in John Deming's Tavern—usually at the licensed inn offering the broadest hearth and the most adequate bar. The Judges met in a kind of mock formality, with little attempt to disassociate the affairs of court from the domestic scene in which they were cast. The dignity was preserved in the tone of voice, the bearing of the principals, and the lingo of the Clerk: "A Commission appointing the Honorable John Strong, Esq. Chief Judge and Gamaliel Painter and Hiland Hall, Esq. side judges was read before the County Court within and for the County of Addison, and they being present took their seats on the Judge's bench."

For eight years, between 1787 and 1795, Painter took the appropriate seat. The session lasted from three days to several weeks depending on the vices of the populace, their animosities and their receptivity to settlement out of court. Everyone was everyone's neighbor, knew the other's business better than his own, and was generous with his ideas on amnesty. The gossipers seldom agreed with the judges or jury, but justice usually prevailed despite their opinions.

Court sessions followed the same pattern year after year. The Judges took their seats. The Justices of the Peace were announced: "*A Commission appointing Nathan Morley, . . . William Brush, John Chipman, . . . Esquires, Justices of the Peace of the County of Addison for the present year . . .*" The long list of tavern keepers was read: "*Timothy Spaulding of Panton licensed to keep a tavern and acknowledged himself recognized to the Treasurer of Addison County that*
118

*he duly observe all the Laws of this State respecting tavern
keepers or houses of public entertainment in the sum of £30.
Hiland Hall Esq. of Cornwall, etc. recognized to the Treasurer
of Addison County in the sum of £30 according to Law . . ."*
and a dozen others, including acknowledgements for Leicester, Bridport, Shoreham, Weybridge, several for Addison and
four for Cornwall. Then, having dispensed with the pre-
liminary formalities, the Court proceeded with the trial
docket.

Most of the cases dealt with delinquent payments in debts,
squabbles over boundary lines, failure to carry out agreements
for delivery of goods, and the expected quota of thefts, misdemeanors and trespass:

> The Plaintiff . . . promised to deliver unto Mr. William
> Hawlet on his order 67 gall. of good W. I. Rum . . .

> The Plaintiff complains and says that the defendant . . .
> with force of arms . . . did with like force cut, take, carry
> away and destroy about three acres of the Plaintiff's good
> wheat then and there standing and growing on said land to
> the value of £20 all of which wrong doing of the Defendant
> are against the peace . . .

> Samuel Pierce, Constable of Salisbury complains . . . that
> the said Stephen Olin and Samuel Stevens (and others) at
> Salisbury . . . did riotously, wantonly, and tumultuously
> assemble and being so assembled did with clubs, staves, and
> other weapons fall trees, expose mens lives and desturb and
> terrify many of the good subjects then about their lawful
> business, and did also in a wanton and tumultuous manner
> take, threaten and imprison Captain Eliezer Claghorn, Capt.
> James Waterhouse and others to the terror of many of the
> good subjects of this state and other enormities did against
> the Laws of this state and the peace and dignity of the
> same . . .

119

The Plaintiff declares and says that at divers times . . . the defendant with force and arms entered into one certain lott of land . . . and being so entered as aforesaid, the defendant did then and there with his feet destroy by treading down and tear up the land and soil of the plaintiff . . . and did also with like force . . . cut down, fell and destroy about 200 of the plaintiff's good timber trees then and there standing and growing . . .

The cases represented the growing pains of a town emerging from a wilderness, where land had changed hands too frequently, where erecting of fences came slowly, where chance had assembled men of conflicting emotions. They were a hardy group and their entertainment kept as few bounds as their land and their spirit. The Judges accepted this fact, and their penalties were measured accordingly. Popular defendants often found themselves officially guiltless; disagreeable plaintiffs earned little satisfaction; even the Salisbury constable for all his trouble with Stephen Olin saw him fined only a pound for his tumultuous conduct, and Stephen's partner in crime only five shillings.

Painter had opportunity to weigh the morals and virtues of his County associates. He was dealing with bold and fearless men who had a singular disrespect for precedent and a jealous respect for individual rights as they chose to interpret them. Fervor for personal independence led to impatience with any kind of restraint. Their resentment toward law and order which limited their independence was frank and fierce.

Such a clientele offered fertile opportunity to any enterprising lawyer who could cope with the climate and match wits with the worst. And Addison County drew them. Painter knew as many as a dozen of them intimately during his service on the bench: Judge Strong of Addison whose only knowledge of law came from legislative assemblies, conventions, and town meetings where he had helped write the law; Henry Olin of Leicester, an enormous man with an enormous memory, quick-witted, well-read, and totally lacking in any formal legal training; Samuel Chipman of Vergennes, admitted to the bar in 1786 with only a common school background, yet serving as attorney for twelve of the twenty-four cases on the docket during his first session, a man of Painter's pattern engaged in buying up all the lots at the Vergennes falls, as Gamaliel had done at Middlebury; John Graham, law student from Connecticut with considerable experience in England; Seth Storrs, a Yale graduate, former school teacher, and a boarder at John Strong's house where he was seeking the good graces of the Judge and courting his daughter; Samuel Miller, the first lawyer to settle in Middlebury, a courteous, discriminating gentleman whose only legal training had been picked up as an apprentice in Rutland; the eloquent Daniel Chipman, Dartmouth graduate, one of the great American attorneys of his time, already making plans to set up his own law school. No one in Addison County had to go far for competent counsel. The lawyers in town made a good living.

Judge Painter and the County Court had been given broad jurisdiction in a state which was still an independent republic. Virtually all crimes and misdemeanors short of capital offenses came within their power, and the Court knew variety as well as gravity in the charges presented for their consideration:

> George Walker Andrews . . . now confined to the Common Gaol in Middlebury with force and arms one station horse of a Bay Colour . . . and the goods and chattels of John Deming . . . feloneously did steal take and had away . . . to the vile Example of all others in like manner offending against the statutes . . . and against the peace and Dignity of the state . . .

Jemine Pain of Addison . . . your petitioner was lawfully married to the said Benjamin Pain . . . and lived with him as a faithful, obedient wife in the discharge and performance of all the duties injoined in the marriage covenant on her part to be performed for twenty-five years— . . . Without just cause given him by your Petitioner the said Benjamin was guilty of breach of marriage covenant in this namely, that the said Benjamin did . . . at divers times . . . commit the crime of adultery; that the said Benjamin for eight years last past at a great variety of times and for a considerable length of time left and forsook the company and conversation of your petitioner for the company and conversation of another woman . . .

John Mead . . . now confined in the Common Gaol in Middlebury in the said County of Addison, not regarding the good and wholesome Laws of this State but being moved and seduced by his own wicked inclinations and vicious habits —and contriving against all the good Citizens of this State, craftily and falsely to deceive and defraud . . . one piece of money—false, feigned and counterfeit money and Coin of Pewter, lead and other base metals in the likeness and similitude of the good, legal, and current money and silver coin of the State of Vermont called Dollars, then and there wickedly, falsely and deceitfully did Make, forge, Counterfeit and Coin against the Statute in such Case made and provided and against the peace and Dignity of the State of Vermont.

Edward Davis of Whiting . . . was voluntarily, wickedly and unlawfully in bed with one Hannah Butler, a single woman, he, the said Edward then and there being the husband of another woman and being so in bed as aforesaid he the said Edward was then and there found against the Statute, . . . and against the peace and dignity of the State.

Despite the Puritan background of these men and women of Addison, they took liberties with the ten commandments as well as with the more voluminous law of the State of Vermont. Suits for fraud, larceny, adultery, arson, slander, wilful destruction, impiety were all on the books. Judge Painter was solicitous of the ethics and rectitude of the freeholders, solicitous of the spiritual welfare of his neighbors, solicitous of the peace and dignity of the state. But after every Court session he was deeply impressed with the need at Middlebury for a Pastor. He was more interested in corrective measures to suppress vice than in dispensing penalties after the deed was done. The spiritual support of a church society was the agent auxiliary to the Court most needed to subdue transgressors. Few disagreed with him that religion was to be regarded as essential to the highest interest of the State, or that suffrage should not be extended to those who failed to attend church. Services, however, were too irregular to put conviction into practice and too irregular to make a religious organization responsible for moral laxity.

The need for a church was desperate, and though the townsfolk had to express admiration for Painter's unwavering tenacity, they did not realize they were closer to getting a temporary one when a special committee of the Legislature finally reported that the situation had been viewed, that all parties concerned had been heard, and they begged leave to report that "the place where the Courthouse and Gaol ought to be Erected and Setting of the Courts Established forever . . . is,—for the Courthouse at a stake by us affixed for that purpose in Middlebury near Middlebury Falls about the center of a square lot of Land lying North of and adjoining the Dwelling house of Gam.[1] Painter . . ."

And then, as though the Almighty were fatigued from the bickering over where He was to be worshipped and sought revenge for the waywardness of his frontier disciples, a season of disaster swept over Middlebury. The year was 1790. Crop failure had laid destitute many of the communities of northern Vermont and southern Canada in the summer of 1789. Starving settlers had straggled into Middlebury for help. They had been treated sympathetically and generously. In fact, Middlebury had been so unsparing in its contributions of food that supplies were dangerously depleted. But the plague moved south in 1790. Winter lasted into May, and crops were slow. Many a household measured out its last ounce of meal before their wheat was knee-high and long before the corn was coming into tassel. Wild life moved to better pasture on the upper slopes of the mountains out of range of hunters. Famine was a new thing in this wilderness where one was accustomed to live off the land and from the bounty of game, but it was real. All the hardships which were common to the North during the previous summer were now sapping the life of Addison County. "I have heard, I have read of famines," reported Nathan Perkins, "but never saw one before, or was in ye midst of one . . . A day of calamity and famine, dearness of truck and want of bread in all their dwellings. It is supposed by ye most judicious & knowing that more than ¼ part of ye people will have neither bread nor meat for 8 weeks, and that some will starve . . . I have mourned with ye inhabitants. Several women I saw had lived four or five days without any food, and had eight or ten Children starving around them, crying for bread & ye poor women had wept till they looked like ghosts. Many families have lived for weeks on what ye people call Leeks—a sort of wild onion— very offensive to me—it poisons all ye milk & Butter of ye settlement, while ye Cows go in ye woods."

But it was this poisonous combination of leeks and milk on which many of Painter's neighbors survived during the

124

early summer months. Children were sent off to the woods to gather the wild onions and bring them home in armfuls to be cooked into soup or eaten as salad along with their bowls of milk. Desperate housewives harvested the inner layer of the bark of oak trees to boil up as stock for unpalatable consommé. Men tramped the forest for days in search of game only to return empty handed. Silent, hungry family groups assembled here and there along the stream beds of the Otter and Lemon Fair with their willow rods and bait. "Such as had strength went to the creek, built a fire, and, as they caught the fish, threw them into it, which yet showing signs of life, and when sufficiently cooked stripped off and ate the flesh, without disturbing the entrails."

When his family became entirely destitute of any kind of flour or meal, John Chipman set out on foot for Ticonderoga and returned days later with a sack of grain over his shoulder. The family lived on milk in the interim. Before the wheat was ripe, women went into the fields and cut off the heads of the grain, dried them, shelled out the wheat and boiled the cereal. Most families lived for weeks without grain of any kind. Even the kitchen shelves at Demings' were empty, and the tavern keeper's family were subsisting on two meals a day, "and after the cows were milked at evening, they finished the day with milk punch, seasoned with a small allowance of whiskey." Deming finally brought in from Lanesborough three pack horses laden with beans, wheat, and corn, and his wife recalled years later that "the sight of such a treasure was an occasion of great triumph."

The sources of supply were far distant; the roads had been little improved since the Revolution; and few of the settlers had capital to make wholesale purchases as Deming had. The whole economy of the Vermont settlements was based on every family's producing its own food. Even with charity on the part of those who had a reserve in their bins and barrels, there was still not enough to go around. The famine, like pestilence, spared no one. It respected neither position nor property. Gamaliel had been more than liberal in making contributions to those in need. His grown sons, Samuel and Joseph, were as hungry as their friends. But it was Mrs. Painter who was most affected, though she had written uncomplainingly to her sister late in January: "I have nothing of note to write. Our family together with your friends at the place are in comfortable state of health . . ." She did not confess that she had been ill during the winter, and that her ailment carried on into the spring. The years of strain had sapped her strength and brought premature age upon her. She was only forty, but her resistance had gone. The proper food that could have helped her now was not available. As the famine advanced, she weakened steadily. The will to live and the tokens of affection brought from every corner of the county were not sufficient to make up for the inadequate subsistence. On April 21, 1790, at the height of the famine, she died quietly and incredibly in the home at the Falls she had labored with Gamaliel to create.

There was no mortician to care for the body; no clergyman to give blessing at a funeral; there was not even a road over which the deceased could be carried to the cemetery at the south end of the town. A pontoon raft was hastily assembled by fastening boards athwart two canoes, and on it the homemade coffin was placed. The craft, carrying the mourners and a crew of friends to propel the boats, began its slow journey up the Otter. The townspeople made up a solemn procession along the shore trail. To add emergency to the pathos, halfway along the journey the overloaded canoes began to leak, and the mourners were obliged to remove their shoes and use them as bails against foundering. The body was laid to rest without benefit of clergy near the site of the first Painter cabin.

To assuage his grief, Judge Painter plunged more deeply than ever into expansion of his business interests and into his work for the community. The yield from crops during the summer and fall was far from bountiful, but it was adequate to stem the effects of the famine. From sales of property, from services as surveyor, from a thriving business at his mills, he was accumulating resources substantially large by Middlebury's standards, and with Ira Allen as partner he had been investing small sums of money in huge tracts of land in the Winooski valley, land, he was sure, that would pay handsome dividends in years to come. He was interested too, in Ira's project for establishing a State University at Burlington and in 1789 had been appointed by the Assembly to receive "absolute donations and particular subscriptions for the use of a College." Painter was becoming a power in the State. His business kept him away from Middlebury for days at a time, but his responsibilities at home never suffered neglect.

A few weeks after his wife's death he was at last named as chairman of a Committee to find a pastor who would settle in Middlebury. The Judge was getting a reputation as a man who got things done. With depression settling over the region and men looking into their consciences for a reason why they should be visited with near disaster from famine, the time was ripe for bringing a mediator into their midst to show them the error of their ways. Painter accepted the chairmanship, hoping that the right pastor might be instrumental in selecting the proper site for the meetinghouse. Less than two weeks later, however, the old, ugly question popped up again. There were those who felt that a pastor should have an orthodox pulpit from which to preach, and that meant deciding on the location of the church before getting the pastor. The dissenters were a majority; they voted to build a meetinghouse but added as a rider that a committee be chosen "to fix on a place to set the meetinghouse." Five committeemen, representing as many factions, were elected to struggle over the issue. Painter was a member, but so were John Chipman and Daniel Foot. Disregarding the second purpose of the appointment, the Judge put his energies and quietest diplomacy into the job of finding a pastor, and in less than six months he had an acceptable candidate. As an afterthought a Congregational society was at last organized, and a week later a temporary pastor took up residence, but not at the Falls.

Painter's public interests, however, during 1790 and 1791 were as much devoted to affairs of State as affairs of Church and Court. After three decades of wrangling over possible annexation by New Hampshire, possible annexation by New York, re-affiliation with Great Britain, and remaining an independent republic, Vermonters and their antagonists were in the throes of a culminating decision. New York and New Hampshire had at length been forced to conclude that the Green Mountains would never be theirs. The mysterious and exploratory negotiations of the Allen brothers to convert Vermont into a dominion of Great Britain had petered out, and Ethan was less willing than he had once been to defend the independence of Vermont by retiring with his "hardy Green Mountain Boys into the desolate caverns of the mountains and wage war with human nature at large." Congress was

128

ready to consider the admission of the aggressive little Republic into the Union.

Painter was serving on an Assembly Committee to make arrangements to buy back from New York all of its claims to Vermont, and penurious as he was with public funds, he was one of the legislators who voted "Yea" in October 1790 on the resolution recommending that the legislature "pay the State of New York thirty thousand dollars" in settlement of the land grants which Yorkers still felt they were entitled to in Vermont. He was one of those who voted affirmatively on an act "authorizing the people of this State to meet in Convention, deliberate upon, and agree to the Constitution of the United States." The convention met on January 6, 1791, and five weeks later President Washington had signed the act which Painter had fought for, argued and lived for: "Be it enacted by the Senate and House of Representatives of the United States of America in Congress assembled, and it is hereby enacted and declared that on the fourth day of March, One Thousand Seven Hundred and Ninety-one, the said State, by the name and style of the 'State of Vermont', shall be received and admitted into this Union, as a new and entire member of the United States of America."

Vermont made the fourteenth state, and Judge Painter gave up his citizenship in an independent republic for that of the United States.

7 INDUSTRIALIST

He had seen it in Connecticut, in Pennsylvania, in New York, in Massachusetts: a town of any importance clung to the spot where nature provided water power. An inland settlement soon shrank to a nonentity if it did not have a falls, a dam or a sluice to bring it industry. Water power meant a mill and a factory; a factory brought trade and people, wealth and a decent livelihood. All things were possible to those who had water power; the future of America—and Middlebury—was in water power. Painter had rights to the Falls and knew how to make the most of their potentialities. The artificer of the Revolution was an artificer for life. He intended to place his talents and his convictions at the disposal of the public, but first he had to convert that public to his philosophy. It was his mission.

Painter was obstinate, inflexible, dogmatic. He could see clearly only his own point of view, but the point of view was magnanimous. He was determined that the public should accept his ideas for their own good. His selfishness was big-hearted; his achievement was for the benefit of the community.

To be sure, he was not neglecting the future of his sons. They were brought up in his philosophy of service; given the best schooling Middlebury offered, but subjected to the only discipline he knew, the harsh discipline of experience. He was devoted to them, and they were his companions on surveying expeditions and business ventures; they were part of his audience at official functions; through participation they were learning the trades he knew. To Samuel eventually would go the management of the mills, and he was already serving his apprenticeship there. To Joseph would go some of his other business interests as soon as he could develop a little of the determination and resolve his brother possessed. But what Painter accomplished by way of creating industry would be their legacy ordained for the benefit of the community. If there was any element of self interest in his enterprises it was for the sake of the boys. In them he instilled his stubborn belief in the value of trade, industry and water power. They were involved in his gamble at the Falls.

The idea of a village at the Falls began to catch on as early as 1788, and realists who convinced themselves that the Painter dream was not entirely empty started approaching him to talk over terms for purchase of house or business lots. The realtor was confident enough in the value of his land not to appear over eager to part with a square rod of it. He had an opportunity to choose who his fellow villagers were to be, and made the most of it. He was interested in taking on as neighbors only those who had the right cut for his design of a community, and he was a discerning judge of character. In his hands he held the future of a village society.

It took considerable imagination to picture on the edge of the Otter a New England village which would match the pleasant towns of Connecticut known to most of the settlers. The Falls area was anything but prepossessing in appearance: a few scattered houses peering out of the edge of the forest on both sides of the Creek, several ramshackle huts, Painter's grist and sawmills on the Middlebury side, Foot's mills on the Cornwall side, gloomy forest to the west and a few acres of fallen timber on the east bank blanketing what Painter optimistically chose to call a Commons. The footing was uncertain everywhere, and everything tended to slide toward the banks of the river. Where timber had been cut, already unsightly second growth was pushing up several feet high to cover the decay. But above the roar of the falls sounded the rumble of a busy gristmill and the screech of sawmills. Intermittently teams jostled through the clay swamps on either side of the stream, eased down the steep incline of rutted highway, and rumbled cautiously over the bridge to deliver grain or pick up lumber at the mills. One of the Painter boys was usually around to lend a hand or exchange pleasantries on the weather if Painter himself was occupied elsewhere. Whether or not the visitors cared to identify it as such, industry had found Middlebury, and Painter let it be known that he would welcome on his land other industry, or tradesmen to feed the industry.

One of his first deeds went to Benjamin Gorton, a New York merchant who had announced his intention of establishing a store in Middlebury. It was a minuscule plot adjoining the bridge, the ideal location for Gorton's interests. But Benjamin never arrived to put the business in operation. Instead, he delegated an enterprising nephew, Jabez Rogers, to explore the possibilities, and Rogers lost no time in setting up the first store in the County. Supplies of dry goods, hardware, and modest quantities of groceries came in over the long route from Lake Champlain landings, and the customers came almost as fast as the supplies. There was more barter in produce at the store than cash trade, but the establishment of such a trading post at Middlebury did almost as much to anchor the center at the Falls as a church could have.

Rogers, however, did not stop with his store. Shortly he set up one of the industries vital to every New England frontier town, a potash plant. To this, farmers could bring cart loads of ashes from the forests they were ravaging to get rid of the trees. The plant converted the ashes into concentrated potash, a light, marketable product which could easily be shipped out to help supply the unlimited demand required for the manufacture of textiles, glass and soap in the industrial centers of England and New England. It was a cash crop that paid for the incidental construction costs of many a settler's frame house in the Vermont backwoods. As still another sideline of the Gorton-Rogers interests Jabez added a makeshift distillery to save farmers the trouble of converting their own grain into liquor, multiplying the local production of alcoholic beverage and leading one of his townswomen to the questionable conclusion: "We had a quiet township of people until Jabez Rogers built his still house."

Professional men were needed, and it took a minimum of Painter's persuasion to coax them to set up their practice in the proper location. In the fall of 1789 he deeded a half acre lot to Samuel Miller, who had just completed a law apprenticeship in Rutland and was looking for a suitable practice to supplement his income as amateur surveyor. To Dr. Matthews in the same year went the lot adjacent to Miller's; Darius Matthews did not have a medical degree, but he had shown such virtuosity in the study of medicine under a physician at Tinmouth that he was licensed to practice at the age of twenty-one. Two years in the profession at Salisbury convinced Painter that he was the practitioner Middlebury needed, and Painter convinced Matthews. To John Deming, an experienced blacksmith, went a full ten acres with the hope that John would bring his way the horseshoeing trade and forging, but the blacksmith did even better than Painter had anticipated. By 1790 he not only had set up his smith shop but also built the first two-story house in the region, a rude mansion with a capacity for twenty-five guests, which was immediately labelled a tavern. The ingenious cabinet maker, William Young, arrived in search of a place to ply his trade, and Painter readily parted with the lot next to Dr. Matthews.

Month by month Middlebury became more completely self-reliant. The town had its own trading post, a gristmill and sawmill; it could heal its sick, repair its equipment, produce its own furniture, provide legal counsel, entertain transients hospitably, and keep up its morale with homemade spirits. "In April 1793," reported Jabez Rogers, "I counted every building of Middlebury Falls and found the number to be 62."

The booming village was now as frequently called Painter's

Mills as Middlebury Falls. The buildings were still mostly of logs, but they were occupied by families of which the father of the town could be justly proud: John Willard, who had survived the torture of impressed British naval service to become a physician and a student of the classics; Festus Hill, a first-class carpenter; the promising lawyer, Daniel Wyman; Sam Mattocks, another tavern keeper; Oliver Brewster, the village tailor; Captain Josiah Fuller, who had given up his military honors to operate a tannery; Erastus Hall, saddler and harness maker; Elias Wilder, the hatter. And new merchants, tavern keepers, and blacksmiths, seeing the possibilities, soon brought competition to those already established. Land frequently changed hands a second time, and plots were subdivided, but Painter had the gratification of seeing the site he had picked for a village well inhabited. There were poverty and squalor, but there were also ambition and opportunity.

What he contributed industrially was appreciated as much by casual visitors as by townspeople. The noted attorney, traveler, and author, John Andrew Graham was so impressed with Painter's accomplishments that he singled him out for special recognition and reported to London readers in 1797 that: "He is universally esteemed and respected by all who know him."

Painter himself was too busy with his real estate business, his surveying, and innumerable public affairs, to devote a great deal of time to the actual operation of his mills. His speculations in land had reached far beyond the limits of Middlebury, and with Ira Allen he owned thousands of acres in the Winooski Valley, a domain large enough to demand the services of an agent. Unfortunately Ira had gone to Europe and been detained there for months that extended into years; unfortunately the boundaries of the land were not always clear; and

136

most unfortunately the agent he had selected was unscrupulous. Many of the dealings in the land reflected the improbity of his agent, Colonel Jacob Davis, but Painter's reputation remained unchallenged, for records of the negotiations were kept to a minimum. Even his agreements and disagreements with Colonel Davis were verbal, and their business was done verbally, or in brittle notes like the one dated April 3, 1795:

> Sir
>
> on my return from your house I called on General Allen he seamed to think that it would be all to gether gess work to Devide the land without seeing it but agreed that I might sell adjoining to the Land sold sufficient to make up my part reckening of it in Quantity and Quality—And I weash you to sell to any person that wants to purchase and make Good pay . . . you know my want in regard to pay better than I can wright and for your Trouble in the Matter I will make you satisfaction—
>
> > I am Sir   Your most Obediant
> > Honble Servant   Gaml Painter.

Minor tracts of land were acquired through payment of overdue taxes to individuals, vast areas were purchased through speculators in New York and Burlington. One purchase was so great that it was bounded by towns rather than private lines: "South on Orange, West on Montpelier, North on Marshfield, containing ten thousand acres." He owned the entire town of Plainfield for a brief period. And what he bought in terms of hundreds of dollars he sold by parcels in terms of thousands of dollars.

Yet despite these fabulous transactions just over the horizon from Middlebury, what interested him most were measures of grain at his mill, square feet of lumber, square rods of land bordering the Falls. No longer able to operate his mills himself, he had persuaded William Goodrich to give up his humble tavern catering to Creek trade, and take over as his superintendent at the Mills. With the help of Painter's two sons, William did a good business and saw that the law relating to mills and millers was kept to the letter:

> Every owner or occupier of a grist-mill, shall well and sufficiently grind the grain brought to such mill, and may take for the toll, one sixteenth part and no more, of all grain of which the remaining part shall be ground into meal, unless the same be boulted; in which case he shall receive one sixty-fourth part more, in addition to such toll; and one thirty-second part of malted grain, the remainder of which shall be ground. And every owner or occupier of a mill, who shall take or exact more toll than is before directed, shall for every such offense, forfeit and pay the sum of three dollars, to the party injured, recoverable with costs, before any justice of the peace, of the county in which such offense shall be committed.

> . . . Every owner or occupier of a grist-mill, shall provide sealed measure namely, one half-bushel, peck, half-peck, two quart, one quart and one pint, with an instrument, with a plain surface, to strick such measures. And if any owner or occupier as aforesaid, shall make use of any false measures or instrument, he shall be liable to the same penalty and in the same manner, as is provided . . .

Since Painter was the Justice of the Peace as well as the miller, he avoided tangles with the law over the share of grain extracted, kept his measures true, his strickle planed; and both he and Goodrich were well supplied with their toll in every quality of grain from bran to "boulted" buckwheat. Nor were they ever short of lumber for any purpose. Timber was the cheapest natural product of Middlebury. The supply was unlimited, and Painter's mills turned out every shape and dimen-

138

sion from oak beams to pine clapboards. Half the early frame houses in the area were the product of his sawmill.

His only competition came from Foot's mills across the bridge in Cornwall, and the Foot interests were thriving. On his side of the river, a suburb of Cornwall was growing out of the wilderness as fast as was Middlebury. Next to the Foots, the principal property owner on the Cornwall side was Seth Storrs, a good lawyer friend of Gamaliel, who had foreseen that the future for business at the Falls was far more promising than in Addison. Anticipating that the Court would be moved to Middlebury, he sold out in Addison and purchased all the land he could get in Cornwall between the Creek and the hill to the west. His influence was cultural as well as commercial. He was a Yale graduate and for several years had taught school with Timothy Dwight at the Seminary in Northampton. But at heart he was a pioneer, and became attached to Addison County after learning the fine points of frontier law from Judge Strong and marrying his daughter. He was elected the first State's Attorney for the County and held the position virtually uncontested during all the period that Painter served as Judge.

Industry was as well established on the west side as on the east. In addition to Foot's saw and grist mills, Jonathan Nichols, an ingenious mechanic, set up in 1794 a forge, triphammer, and gun factory. His brother Josiah joined him two years later, and the two developed one of the best forging businesses in the State. Captain Ebenezer Markham, who had been "committed to the liberties of the Middlebury jail" for inability to pay his debts, improved his time by establishing the first nail factory in the State. Middlebury had a silversmith on the east side, Cornwall had a goldsmith on the west. Cornwall had its own taverns, a competent fuller and dresser of cloth in Harvey Bell, a clothier, a tannery, a potash plant, and two or three merchants who were not doing as well as the merchants across the Creek.

And when the competition was beginning to reach a peak, the proposal was cautiously circulated that a merger of the two villages would make a superior industrial center. The bridge should connect rather than divide. It was a proposition typical of Gamaliel Painter, who had been superintending the job of reflooring that bridge with oak planks. There was behind-scenes politicizing; there was deft argumentation; there were quiet campaigns. The idea had merit. Capital was made of the fact that Cornwall had located its church four miles from the orphan settlement at the Falls. Cornwall had already helped to pay for two bridges across the Creek, bridges that benefited Middlebury principally. Most of the land west of the Creek was miry swamp unsuited for expansion of the village, and the long stretches of road contemplated across the swamps both to the south and west could only mean heavier taxes for Cornwall citizens to the benefit of Middlebury citizens.

It took less than a year to carry the issue. The proposal was officially presented at a Cornwall town meeting in December, 1795. Action was tabled until the following fall. Dissidents argued over details as to just where the new boundaries would fall, whose farms would be cut in half. In early October of 1796 the freemen had an opportunity to vote on whether as much as two thirds of Cornwall would secede, but a compromise was made, and late that same month the General Assembly approved an act annexing the northeasterly part of the Town of Cornwall to the Town of Middlebury.

The action took place so quickly and so quietly that few, except men like Seth Storrs, Gamaliel Painter and the Foots, appeared to have any realization of its significance. With hardly a petition or a resolution, Middlebury had grabbed the most valuable corner of Cornwall, doubled its own potentialities, and for all time Cornwall had lost any possibility of being more than a sprawling rural township. Residents at the Falls, on both sides of the bridge, congratulated themselves on having perpetrated a masterstroke, and people of Cornwall a century later were still wondering how it happened.

Gamaliel Painter's scheme of establishing a major community had surpassed even his original intentions. For practically all of the industrial as well as the political ventures he had furnished counsel if not capital. He was totally unread in political and economic theory, but he had common sense which put the most logical and fundamental theory to practice. He unhesitatingly invested his own funds in any commercial enterprise that had reasonable prospects of success. Inevitably he made money. On his local investments the returns were not large, but they were sufficient to reward him liberally for his exertions and his perspicacity.

On two occasions when inns were needed, he turned tavern keeper in partnership with John Deming and John Chipman, paid the statutory fee of thirty pounds, and was officially licensed by the court in which he was a judge to operate "houses of public entertainment for one year from the rising of such court," and was thereby required by law "at all times to be furnished with suitable refreshments, provisions and accomodation for travelers, their cattle and horses, on penalty of forfeiting the sum of three dollars." He was required to "put up a proper sign upon or near the front of his house with his name thereon, and to erect and keep in good repair a good and sufficient shed or covering for horses, near his house, with a suitable trough or manger, convenient for the accommodation of travelers' horses." His bar was adequately protected from those who attempted to sell liquor without license: "If any person or persons not having a licence to keep an inn or house of public entertainment . . . shall presume to become a common inn keeper or keeper of a house of public entertainment, or shall publicly or privately sell any wine, rum, brandy, or other strong liquors, metheglin, strong beer, ale, or cyder, by a less quantity than one quart of wine, rum, brandy or other strong liquors, or by a less quantity than one gallon of metheglin, strong beer, ale, or cyder, he . . . shall forfeit and pay for the first offense a fine of ten dollars . . ." The only exception to this law came on days of "general muster, and other public and proper occasions" when the selectmen had authority to grant anyone power for three days "to mix and sell any of the liquors aforesaid."

But even with its half dozen well-provided taverns, the greater prestige of a community stretching across the Creek, and the increased commercial population at Middlebury Falls, indecision still prevailed on the location of the church, and until a spire gave ecclesiastical approval to the center, the town might yet become divided. Unable to make progress on the church structure, Painter renewed his determination to erect an edifice that would at least identify Middlebury as the shire town.

The lot on which the State authorities had placed a stake to designate the location of the Courthouse was still nothing but a site. The only semblance of a building on it was a rough wooden structure labeled "Addison County Gaol." Painter had helped design and erect the building under pressure of state law and urgent need, but it was nothing to be proud of.

142

It contained a dungeon, a number of cool, stoutly-guarded cells for prisoners, and a tenement for the jailor's family. But less civic-minded citizens than the Judge recognized the disgrace of having a jail without a courthouse. Other shire towns of the State, with smaller populations, had afforded substantial courthouses and had brought the badge of respectability to their communities by entertaining the State Legislature in them. It was a matter of pride with other progressive towns. It should be a matter of pride for Middlebury. The public could not ignore much longer Painter's gift of the choicest site on his lands "for the express use and purpose of erecting a Court House and jail thereon, and as a common, never to be divided or put to any other use." This was land that could have been sold for a substantial price, and the price Painter was commanding for his lots was well known in all corners of the County. Men who most suspected his usual motives found little reason for suspicion here. The cause of the courthouse was good. A few progressives even had the courage to make what they thought was a novel suggestion—that it might provide a desirable substitute for Foot's barn as a meetinghouse. And perhaps Painter was right, the roving Legislature might accept an invitation to use Middlebury as the capital for a year. County citizens joined with Middlebury citizens in demanding a courthouse that would measure up to any in the State.

They could not afford a pretty building, but it would be dignified in proportion, ample in size, and substantial in construction. Painter's plans were accepted. It took two years to execute them, but as the building rose in 1797 and 1798, community self-respect mounted. The white edifice with its belfry could have easily passed for a church. The high windows on the sides, the plain entrance, and the semicircular window in the pediment all contributed to the appearance of a church rather than a courthouse. The interior was one large room with slanting floor, the pews and benches facing the low platform; a gallery in the rear. The ceiling was arched, two stories in height, and the whole building utterly impractical from the point of view of those concerned with winter temperatures. Fireplaces could never begin to take either the March or November chill from the interior, and the Courts decided early that they preferred the warmth and comfort of Deming's tavern to the spaciousness and dignity of the courthouse. But since a reasonable amount of suffering was expected of churchgoers, the Congregational Society decided to adopt it without dispute; meetings could be held there; and social assemblies, dimly lighted by candle sconces, could put up with the cold.

Painter had a new partner to share his enthusiasms now. In 1795 he had made a trip back to Salisbury, Connecticut, and, after a respectable interval and a quiet ceremony in the home of the Justice of the Peace, had returned with a second wife. Victoria was as plain and inelegant as her husband, but what she lacked in charm and gentility she more than made up in strength of character, sociability, and unaffected fluency of speech. She was far better educated than Gamaliel, was sympathetic or tolerant toward all the causes he espoused, and was discriminating in her household tastes. Middlebury accepted her with hearty approval, and although Gamaliel was in his upper fifties and she only thirty-five, the gossips were charitable in their commentary. To everyone the first lady shortly became known as "Vicca," even to her stepsons who more nearly approximated her age than did their father. She was a good hostess, equal to the variety of occasions in which her husband was constantly involving himself, and at once he made plans

144

to build her a home that would more nearly symbolize her station in the community. In contrast with other residences in town it would be a palace: a square, three-storied house with fine doorways, fine cornices, fine roof lines. There would be at least a dozen rooms, each with a handsome fireplace and many windows; beautiful hallways and a graceful spiral staircase. It would stand on the highest point of land near the Falls, with a view of the Green Mountains to the east, the winding Otter and the Adirondacks to the west.

Painter, who had begun to have a hesitation in his walk before the marriage, had a new burst of youth. Into his household Vicca brought an animation, an eagerness, and a spark of humor that had long been missing. All four members of the family might have been of the same age, yet Vicca was a good mother, a good companion, and a liberal education to her stepsons. Samuel and Joseph had profited by as much schooling as the settlement offered; they expressed themselves well, were well-mannered and well-disciplined, but both, at heart, were frontiersmen. Vicca softened a callousness they had developed in the five years without a mother. And the following year they were presented with a sister, Abby Victoria, who became the fondling of the whole family. "We have," Samuel wrote to his Aunt Hannah Sheldon in Salisbury when Abby was less than four months old, "a fine little Sister that makes a great addition to our family felicity and promises much future satisfaction." Then he added a sly confession of interest in his cousin Esther who was visiting in Middlebury: "I have, Aunt Hannah, become very steady and want nothing but a Wife to make me completely domesticated and I hope happy. Esther is very hearty and is almost a Woman . . ."

Samuel, however, was never betrothed to Esther; unheralded

145

catastrophe halted the romance. On June 28th, with Samuel Southworth, the district schoolteacher, Samuel was a leader in the Masonic procession to the Courthouse commemorating St. John's Day. The interior of the building was not completed, but Reverend Ball had been engaged to come up from Rutland to give an address, an ambitious choral program had been arranged, and the Courthouse was the only shelter large enough to accommodate the expected throng. Samuel led the singing. "All was lovely and gay," wrote Victoria, "and much the largest number of people were collected that have ever been together since I lived in the place. They met for the first time in the Courthouse . . . The singers had been very ambitious to learn tunes suitable to the day. The Ladies who sang were all dressed in white. They assembled at our house and were escorted from thence to the Court House by Mr. Southworth, Sam and some other young men. Everything conducted with propriety and good order."

The service was at eleven. At two that afternoon Samuel was dead. Gamaliel, in his fumbling grammar, gave the details in a letter to his brother-in-law in Salisbury:

> If possible I will calm my troubled mind and give you a history of the different vicissitudes of life that has past in my family. . . . On Wednesday of last week I received an invitation to dine at Major Chipman's . . . Just as we was about to set off Mr. Southworth came . . . This Mr. Southworth was son to Judge Southworth of Mayfield in Connecticut studying law with Col. Storrs of this place about 25 years of age a person of a most eminent character . . . I took Mrs. Painter Esther & my little infant Abagail in the waggon and rode to Major Chipmans left Mr. Southworth Sama & Hannah at my house. after dinner walked out in the garden and after taking a view of the works of Nature and art was returning to the house saw Esqr Miller riding

full speed whose looks bespoke distress he informed me that Mr. Southworth was drowned at the half mile bridge and was taken out of the water before he came away and that he was afraid that Sama was drowned as they did not know where he was and did not know but he might go to bath with him.

That was all the information that he gave me Jumped into the waggon and after riding near two miles with out there being a word spoke I told Mrs. Painter that Samas fate was determined She spoke as though she thought I was hasty in my declaration saying that Esqr. Miller gave no such information I told her that Esqr Miller had had time to reflect and had given such information as he thought prudent, when we arrived at my house found it surrounded with people when we entered the door found Sama a lifeless corps but not withstanding there had been and were still using every means in the human art to restore life but to no effect. You can better conceave the distress of my family than I can describe it.

I should be glad to acquaint you of the circumstances of the matter but it is out of my power for we do not know them ourselves . . . Mr. Southworth continued at my house some time after I left it. Sama and he had some conversation concerning going to the creek to bath one says to the other the weather was so very hot that thought he would be prediditial to their health the other for answer says that they had not been exercising and their blood was cool. They went off and agreed to return in about an hour to dine the next that was heard (which was about an hour after) was the cry of people drowning and every person running to the place not knowing who until their cloath was found. There was a man fishing on the opposite side of the creek and saw them go into the water but directly went off and left them and heard no more of them. There was two men coming down the creek in a boat and heard somebody hollow. they soon got round a point of land and saw a man swimming towards the shore and they say they did not think of anything being the matter but after a while called to him saying are you drowning and he sunk. They run the boat right over where he lay which was not the length of the boat from shore and the water about seven feet deep one of them sit down on the bank of the creek to appearance as senseless as a brute. Mr. Southworth all the while in plain sight while the other went half a mile to call help and by account it was not half a minute after the first men that arrived & started in to the boat before he had Mr. Southworth out of the water. To human appearance these two fellows might of saved Mr. Southworth much easier than I can give you the account. They give an account of Sama. he was found near the middle of the creek where the water was 20 feet deep. How it all happened to be God only knowes. we never expect to get any further information. The two men that was in the boat are strangers have been here but a short time. They have been under examination and it is generally agreed that they had no design but were stupid senseless creatures I can say for myself that I never have reflected on these men although their conduct appears unaccountable and may serve to shew that every thing is calculated to bring about the design of the Supreme being and that it is out of the power of all the human species to counter act any thing supreme . . .

It took a stout constitution and firm faith for Gamaliel to accept the fate of his son with such resolution. Samuel was twenty-five, and at the time Painter was engaged in reconstructing and enlarging his mills with the prospect of turning over their operation to him. Of the two sons, Samuel possessed the greater sense of responsibility and the greater adaptability to business enterprise. All of Painter's plans had included forethought for them. The death of Samuel, his favorite son and the shrewdest, affected him profoundly and disrupted his whole design for the future. He completed the reconstruction of his mills, but he no longer had the will or the heart to manage them. They were Sama's mills and with Sama gone, the

148

mills must go. They were haunted with the memory of Samuel. At the first opportunity he disposed of both the saw and grist mills, because Sama was still there. His interest in industry for Middlebury never faltered, but he would have no further personal part in it.

8 EDUCATOR

The man responsible for founding the first college to open its doors in Vermont did not have the remotest bid to anything approaching erudition. Painter was unread and uncultivated. The only formal education he possessed was a few broken years of common schooling in Salisbury, Connecticut. He read haltingly; he wrote laboriously. As a conversationalist he was pauciloquent; as a public speaker he was colorless and so painfully dull that he was never invited to address a gathering where the oratory was expected to be anything but deliberative or platitudinous. He was at home where he could be persistent or factual. When his supporters wanted a job done that called for slowly wearing down an audience with figures, facts and homely wisdom, Painter was chosen.

His education was in the school of humanity. Some of the wisdom which the scholars and the skilled, with whom he associated, had acquired in years of book learning, he acquired in larger measure from first-hand experience. A discipline they had secured in literary pursuits, he was forced to secure the harder way by working with men. What they may have read about, he had seen. He was a self-made philosopher, economist and theologian, even though he lacked the vocabulary to let others know what he knew.

In the experience with his own two sons he had been brought face to face with the difficulty of finding adequate facilities for formal education very far north of New Haven, except at young institutions like those at Williamstown and Hanover. He recognized the deficiencies in his sons' schooling, and in his; he recognized also the fallibility of exposure to the school of experience. His boys had learned their R's in Furnace Village, at the dingy schoolhouse in the southern end of town and in the scarcely better environment of the makeshift common schools run seasonally by Mrs. Goodrich and Mr. Southworth at the Falls. Painter had helped to create the state statutes which required towns to set up district schools, but if Middlebury were to fulfill its educational obligations, what it needed most was a good central academy to supplement the district school and carry on from where it left off.

He talked over his ideas with Seth Storrs, now a staunch campaigner for Middlebury on the other side of the bridge. Seth had had actual experience in academy teaching and knew more about education than anyone else in town. He not only concurred with Painter, but even volunteered to turn over part of his farm for a schoolyard. He had the ideal location, a swampy acre or two, not much good for farming, about as near to the bridge on the west side as the lands Gamaliel had turned over to the town on the east side. Seth carried his proposition to his neighbors, the Foots, Dr. Matthews and Anthony Rhodes. The Foots and Rhodes were not much interested in education as such, but an adjacent school park would lend to the neighborhood a dignity which was certainly lacking, and ought, at least, to enhance the value of their other real estate. Storrs wanted a good, generous quadrangle for the academy, and eventually he persuaded his neighbors to give up corners of their lots jutting into the area he had hopefully marked off. Other townsfolk with growing children endorsed the idea of the school, and with the procuring of the land a certainty, Painter, the indefatigable lobbyist, was packed off to the State Assembly in the Fall of 1797, with instructions to bring back the charter for a County Grammar School. Samuel Miller and Daniel Chipman were already there in other official capacities. "The influence of Painter with his cunning, Chipman with his argument, and Miller with his courteous address," claimed a competing politician, "if it were possible, would deceive the very elect."

On the ninth of November, word came back from Windsor that the cunning, the argument, and the courteous address had been effective. The trio had not failed their constituents. On the previous day the legislature had yielded. Middlebury had a grammar school on paper—and a challenge. Celebrating citizens proudly pored over the rough copy of the statute to discover the full tenor of the challenge:

> It is enacted by the General Assembly of the State of Vermont, that there be, and hereby is instituted and established, a grammar school, at such place at Middlebury, in the county of Addison, as the corporation herein after named, shall think

153

most convenient for that purpose, to be known and designated by the name of Addison County Grammar School.

And it is hereby further enacted, that Messrs. Gamaliel Painter, Seth Storrs, Samuel Miller, Daniel Chipman and Darius Matthews, and such others, as shall be appointed . . . constitute the board of trustees . . . And the said corporation are hereby . . . appointed a body corporate, and . . . shall have full power to take by gift, grant, purchase, or devise, any estate, either real, or personal, for the use of said grammar school; . . . and also to appoint, elect, support and remove, from time to time all such instructors as they shall find necessary . . .

The school was forever free and exempt from taxes, and the instructors and students were generously exempt from military service as well as from personal taxation. The challenge was tucked into a proviso in the last paragraph of the bill: "Provided always that, the inhabitants of Middlebury aforesaid, and such others as may voluntarily subscribe therefor, shall build and finish a good and sufficient house for said grammar school, of the value of one thousand dollars, by the next stated session of this legislature, and shall forever keep the same in good repair."

Painter had already prepared Middlebury for this clause. He had indoctrinated the townspeople with the fact that the institution they wanted would be expensive. A thousand cash dollars was a sizable sum to be subscribed in a backwoods community, and the crafty Painter smugly withheld the fact that he had well over a thousand in promises before he took the petition to the legislature. By the next spring he had accumulated in property or cash four times the amount the legislature had stipulated. He also had the building well under way, a principal appointed, and a considerable list of students awaiting admission.

The building was a remarkable product of craftsmanship and engineering. The one feature of the exterior that most impressed anyone at first sight was the number of windows. Other buildings in the town had been constructed with a minimum of windows because lumber was cheap and glass was costly. The Grammar School was put up without reference to this limitation. One wondered how the builders had contrived to get so many windows into such a relatively small structure, as if they were obsessed with the idea of letting more than one kind of light into the school. It was three stories high, all of wood, with east and west entries that defied anyone's telling which was the front and which the rear. A cupola on the roof gave it the necessary institutional look, and the whole building, eighty feet in length and half as wide, painted white, stood starkly monumental against the forest to the west.

The inside was compartmented to accommodate all the assorted requirements of a boys' school, with classrooms, laboratory, and library on the first floor, dormitory rooms on the upper two floors, a chapel occupying the central part of the third floor. Each room had a fireplace, and an indigent student gifted at baking corn bread or roasting game could eke out a lean subsistence in the building, though most students preferred the board provided at about a dollar a week by village housewives. Each boy furnished his own water bucket and stood in line at the well near the west entrance to operate the windlass for lavatory and laundry purposes.

The master of the new building was Jeremiah Atwater, a youth from Yale who looked younger than his twenty-four years; and Gamaliel and the other trustees were of necessity called upon frequently to settle disciplinary problems which the undersized Principal could not handle by himself. But Atwater was a qualified instructor in Latin and elocution, algebra and arithmetic, grammar and Greek. He was a protégé of Timothy Dwight. The Yale President had granted him a degree before he was twenty, had recalled him as tutor, and released him to Middlebury with reluctance.

As an antidote for a recurrent ailment, President Dwight took long horseback trips through New England, visiting Yale alumni and gathering at the same time first-hand data for a series of economic geographies to be published in Great Britain. His itinerary was unscheduled, and the august gentleman had a habit of dropping in on his friends without prior warning. In the fall of 1798, Atwater and Seth Storrs were favored with such an unheralded visit. Momentarily the village was thrown into confusion by the appearance of New England's most venerated educator, but the local hierarchy recovered quickly enough to realize that they had in their midst a man whose professional endorsement could be most useful.

The trustees of the Addison County Grammar School had already reached agreement among themselves that their school, with a minimum of effort, could be expanded into a college. Dwight's endorsement of such a step would be worth more than the combined commentary of all the men of letters in the State. The best host in the village was Samuel Miller who had married an inkeeper's daughter, and knew the refinements of gracious entertaining. The Grammar School trustees were hastily assembled in the Miller dining room for a supper worthy of the President of Yale, and over the liqueurs in Miller's adjacent office after the meal, Middlebury College was conceived. Dr. Dwight was as enthusiastic about converting the Grammar School into an institution of higher learning as were Painter, Storrs, Miller or Dr. Matthews. It was practical, it was needed. The conference made a strong enough
156

impression on him so that years later he published the details of it in his New England travelogue: "The evening of the 30th, I spent in company with a number of gentlemen, in a consultation concerning their projected seminary, at the house of S. Miller, Esq. . . . The gentlemen explained to me their own views of the importance of such an institution to their state; the propriety of making this town the seat of it; their own intentions and the wishes of many respectable people in the State . . . When they had unfolded their views, I frankly communicated to them my own, and have since had no reason to complain that they were disregarded."

Dwight was a strategist as well as an educator, and gave professional advice on the best procedure for creating a college: Gamaliel should be given the job of selling the idea to the Legislature; classrooms of the Grammar School would be used for both secondary and higher education; and Jeremiah Atwater, a notable absentee at the conference, could be elevated to the College Presidency.

The 1798 session of the Legislature opened at Vergennes less than two weeks later, but Painter's portfolio was ready. Since Daniel Chipman was the representative from Middlebury that year, strong support could be expected from this fellow-trustee of the Grammar School. However, the agenda for the Session was so filled with matters of greater urgency and more personal interest that the petition was not read until the last day of October. The Assembly was disturbed about subversive foreign influences and was considering a constitutional amendment which would exclude foreign-born citizens from serving in high places; New York Indian tribes were appealing for restoration of their hunting rights in Vermont; and every town in the State was seeking authorization of taxes for roads and bridges. Painter cooled his heels in the Vergennes lobby and had ample time to seek patronage for his bill. Finally, on October 31st, "the petition of Gamaliel Painter, and others, trustees of the Addison County Grammar School," was sandwiched in between debate on authorizing Mooretown to levy a tax of three cents per acre to finance a bridge over the Onion River, and a formal resolution that the Governor investigate the terms of a treaty made between New York and "some of the indian nations." It was given a perfunctory reading and was immediately pushed aside by an order to refer it to a committee, "consisting of one member from each county to be nominated by the Clerk of the House."

The Clerk could scarcely have selected a group of more disinterested men. Most were from remote Vermont towns where allegiance to a cause respecting Middlebury would be foreign. They lived in settlements like Sunderland, Hinsdale, Hartland, Brookfield, Jericho, Lyndon, and St. Albans. The Clerk might at least have appointed from Addison County a lawyer of the calibre of Cornwall's William Slade; instead, Ezra Hoyt from New Haven was chosen. Painter may have done his lobbying too thoroughly. The committee sat on the petition until three days before the Session was to close. Their coolness toward it even crept into the Clerk's minutes:

> The Committee to whom was referred the petition of Gamaliel Painter, and others, trustees of Addison County Grammar School, stating that they have at several thousand dollars expense, erected large and convenient buildings for the accommodation of scholars; they therefore pray the general assembly to establish a college or university at said Middlebury, and grant a charter of incorporation to such trustees, and investing them with such powers, as shall be thought expedient—made report, that the said petition ought

158

to be referred to the next session of the Legislature, for further consideration. Which report being read and accepted, *Ordered*, that the petition be referred to the next session of the general assembly.

The Assemblymen dropped the matter with indifference and proceeded to a resolution calling for wider distribution of copies of the Constitution of the United States to their constituents.

Painter was thoroughly disappointed, but not subdued. His idea, the germ out of which Middlebury College was eventually to grow, had at last been planted with the Legislature. Although his portfolio was filed away for another year, he made use of every opportunity to spread its gospel to the four corners of the State. On the tenth of October, 1799, he put in an appearance for the opening of the Legislature held that year at Windsor. His petition now had the advantage of coming under the head of old business; it was brought to the floor on the third day of the Session and was immediately referred to a committee of seven "to join a Committee from Council, to state facts and make report." Addison County was not even represented in the group this time. Gamaliel returned to Middlebury. For the full length of the session the petition rested with the Committee, and not until late afternoon before the closing day did it come to light. Exactly what happened in 1798 was recorded again in minutes that were beginning to sound like a refrain:

> The Committee to whom was referred a petition of the trustees of Addison County Grammar School, stating, that they and others, inhabitants of the town of Middlebury, have at very considerable expense, erected large and convenient buildings at said Middlebury, suited to the purposes of a college; and praying that the Legislature would establish a

159

college at said town, with such privileges as are common to other similar institutions, made report, that the said bill be referred to the next session of the Legislature. Ordered, that the said report be accepted.

Painter was stunned when he heard the news. He knew now that politics was at work against him. The legislators were stalling; they had previously approved a University at Burlington in Chittenden County, and wanted to give it a chance to get into operation at the expense of Middlebury. If the University actually opened before Middlebury had a college, there would be small chance of its ever being approved. Painter had discussed this quandary with Timothy Dwight, pointing out that, "a college was already incorporated in the State, the intended seat of which was to be Burlington; that it had been incorporated some years and was liberally endowed; but that . . . nothing material had been done toward carrying it into operation; that although some indecisive efforts had been made by the trustees soon after their appointment, all its concerns had, for a considerable time, been at a stand; that there was now less reason to expect any efficacious efforts from those gentlemen than there had been heretofore; as they themselves appeared to have relinquished both exertion and hope." The possibility that the University of Vermont, chartered eight years before, and still without a faculty member or a student, could keep Middlebury from having a college annoyed Painter and his fellow trustees more than they were ready to admit.

The whole question of locating a college in Vermont had been a political hot potato since 1785 when Elijah Paine had offered two thousand pounds to the Assembly if the establishment of a college were authorized at Williamstown in the eastern part of the State a dozen miles south of Montpelier.

160

Paine College failed to materialize on the pretext that "the laudable and generous donations" were insufficient, but the more decisive reason was disagreement on location. In 1789 attempt was again made to persuade the Legislature "to take measures for perfixing on the place for erecting a College," and Painter was named to serve on a committee for collecting donations, but it was Ira Allen who settled the issue temporarily by bidding four thousand pounds if the College were located at Burlington, and by 1791 the Assembly was ready to vote in favor of the General's proposition. But for years the opening of Allen College was delayed while the donor was unable to make good his pledge, and during those years supporters of education in the upper counties of the State lost none of their determination to see the institution located in Burlington.

Painter was well aware of all the intrigue, and in anticipation of having to contend with violent opposition, he was instrumental in persuading the Legislature to meet at the new Courthouse in Middlebury for the 1800 Session. The Assembly would find it more difficult to turn down the proposition of a host town.

By 1800 Middlebury had as much to offer the Assemblymen by way of entertainment as most any other community in the State. There were decent shops, good mills, a few fine homes, some excellent taverns, a respectable Courthouse for session meetings and a citizenry proud enough of its town to provide benevolent hospitality. They arrived to taste that hospitality on Thursday, the ninth of October. Autumn had blossomed its ripest foliage. Every householder had painted a fence, landscaped a yard, graded a stretch of public highway. Flags were out, the most colorful farm produce was on display at the store fronts, candles were in the windows for a big night illumination. The tavern bars were well stocked, and the Courthouse was spick-and-span. Welcome was everywhere. Middlebury was at its best.

Opening formalities took up the best part of Thursday and Friday. New representatives had to take the necessary oaths; the Governor and Council of Censors had to make their reports, impeachment action had to be filed against John Chipman, high sheriff of Addison, "for wittingly and willingly taking and receiving greater fees for services than allowed by law." But early on Saturday morning the legislators were introduced to the familiar "Petition of Gamaliel Painter and others." Again the document was referred to a committee—a more sympathetically chosen committee.

In less than three weeks their report was ready. There was commendation this time for "Gamaliel Painter, and others, trustees of Addison County Grammar School" for their "ardent desire to promote and encourage the education of youth." The committee were in complete agreement on the design for "establishing and carrying into immediate operation, a college or university within this State . . . in said Middlebury." They favored granting "a charter of incorporation to such trustees as shall be appointed, vesting in such trustees such rights and privileges as are enjoyed and exercised by the corporations and trustees of other colleges and universities." In fact, it was the unanimous opinion of the committee that "An act incorporating and establishing a college at Middlebury . . . ought to be passed into a law of this State."

The report was made the order of the day for the following morning. Actually it did not get on the agenda until late the next afternoon. The dissenters from Chittenden County were at work: the State could not support two universities. But legislators were unwilling to overlook the local hospitality, or face their hosts that night with a negative vote. The House resolved itself into a "Committee of the whole house", the candles were lighted, and the Burlingtonians opened up against the Middleburians. It was long after dark before the speaker resumed his chair and Mr. Olin reported formally for the Committee of the Whole the adoption of a resolution, "That it is expedient at this time to incorporate another university in this State."

The tavern barkeepers did a large business that night.

On the following morning the bill was read a second time and the motion made that, "An act incorporating and establishing a college at Middlebury . . . be engrossed and sent to the governor and Council for their revision and concurrence or proposals for amendment." Elnathan Keys, representative from Burlington, demanded that the "yeas and nays be required."

The roll was called. There was not a single favorable vote from the twenty representatives of Chittenden County, and most of the other negative votes were from adjacent Franklin County. But the bill passed with 117 yeas. Painter had at last won his cause.

Isaac Tichenor, Governor and Commander-in-Chief in and over the State of Vermont, issued the Charter of Middlebury College the following day, granting the President and Fellows "the government, care and management of the said College and of all matters and affairs thereto belonging"; granting authority to "establish all such wholesome and reasonable laws, rules, and ordinances, not repugnant to the Constitution, and Laws of this State or the United States as they shall think fit and proper for the instruction and education of the Students";

granting "power to appoint a scribe, or register, a treasurer, tutors, professors, steward, and butler, and such other officers and servants . . . as they shall find necessary and think fit to appoint for promoting good Literature"; granting authority to administer "Oaths, not being contrary to the Constitution"; granting to all regular employees of the College exemption from "all rates, taxes, military service, working on highways, and other such duties and services"; granting and ordaining "that there shall be a general meeting of the President, and Fellows of said College, in the said College House on the first Tuesday of November annually."

The three years of legislative argumentation had stirred up a great deal of enmity against Middlebury, particularly in the northern Lake counties of Chittenden and Franklin which were totally against bringing competition to the University at Burlington, but the argumentation had served as invaluable publicity for the College. It had been confidently noised about that the passage of the bill was inevitable, and on the basis of that confidence, a waiting list of candidates for admission was already on file. The charter was granted on the first Saturday of November, and the first Tuesday in November was only three days off. In compliance with the terms of the charter, a meeting was immediately called for that Tuesday. The charter President, Jeremiah Atwater, was there; Painter was there; Daniel Chipman took leave from the Legislature to put in an appearance, as did the representative from Thetford, Judge Jedidiah Buckingham, and State Councillor Stephen Jacob. All of the original Grammar School trustees had automatically become College trustees, and all arrived at the Grammar School library.

The eight barely made a quorum, but there had not even

164

been sufficient time to inform the other half of the Board that they had been appointed. A Registrar, a Treasurer and a Tutor were elected, and the meeting was adjourned to the next day. Then, on Wednesday, setting an all-time record for expedition in putting a college into operation, the first seven candidates for admission were examined by the Board, and all seven enrolled without qualification, five as freshmen, two as sophomores.

During the examinations Painter sat silent and embarrassed as Atwater and Storrs harassed the students with posers on English grammar, historical chronology, geometry and natural philosophy, and pried into their knowledge of Virgil, Tully and the Greek Testament. After that first exposure to academic standards, the unlearned Gamaliel chose to devote most of his supervision of the College to material affairs.

As the College grew during the following years, he attended frequent exhibitions and enjoyed the student disputations on political and religious affairs. He deplored the vandalism of students and their occasional moral laxity. He watched the finances carefully but preferred to let others pass on the academic qualifications of new students and of new faculty members. He was interested in making arrangements for some sort of Commons for the men so that they would not have to dine in private homes scattered through the community. After the College at Burlington was finally started, he repeatedly served as agent of the Board in appealing to the Legislature for more equitable sharing of the State educational funds and the returns from "college lands" which had been converted from the original Church of England grants to the purpose of State education.

His prejudice against the University of Vermont developed

165

into discreet antagonism. He had no sympathy for a college that would permit its principal benefactor, Ira Allen, to be sued for benefactions which he could now ill afford to contribute. Ira was in desperate circumstances, and when the State persistently made demands he could not meet, he justifiably relinquished his interest in the college he had founded. He had no desire to see his own sons educated there, and when they were ready for college, it was to his friend Gamaliel Painter that he turned for help.

"Herewith, I commit to your care my two sons, Ira and Zimri, whom I intend shall receive an education at Middlebury College," he wrote to Gamaliel and Victoria. " I hope you will not consider them as mere boarders, but as under your immediate care and protection subject to your commands, & particularly that they be enjoined to pay strict attention to their studies, that they be refrained from keeping bad company, from being out late nights and such other vices as boys of their ages are liable to fall into, that they attend public worship and all regulations thought best . . ."

Painter carried out his charge with such austerity that within three months young Ira was complaining to his father, "The place that we board at I do not like." It may have been the confusion of the big household, it may have been because of the rigorous discipline, but Ira tactfully gave as the reason for disliking his residence the tardiness of breakfast "which makes it inconvenient getting our lessons . . . So much time lost puts us back in our studies." He wanted to move nearer the freedom of the campus.

Painter was a martinet in his relations with other college boys as well as the Allens. Lest a student should be unduly influenced by uncertified tutors, he voted with the trustees

166

that "No student in term shall put himself under the instruction of any person not an officer of the College, on pain of admonition, suspension, or rustication"; and lest an undergraduate's immature knowledge unduly influence those in the environs of the College, he voted that "No student without the permission of the President shall publicly exhibit any original or selected composition within five miles of the College." When he observed students in inappropriate local society, he voted that "Any student be prohibited from boarding in the taverns of Middlebury . . . and also that they be prohibited from resorting to any such tavern for liquor or refreshment."

Painter was the principal founder of the College, but in the capacity of educator he devoted most of the rest of his life to the financial welfare of Middlebury, in order that those better qualified might promote larger educational objectives as they saw them, not as he saw them.

9 CHURCHMAN

The Holy Ghost was as real to Gamaliel Painter as was the Father, the Son, and Pastor Thomas Merrill. His Lord was a god of thunder and retribution. His theology was mixed with brimstone, and his religion dominated by a deep feeling that something terrible was going to happen. He believed that the deceased saints resided in "heavenly mansions in the presence of the Lamb," that the wicked lived "in prison, in darkness, in despair, in everlasting torment." He believed that "what rendered the arduous work of the ministry necessary was the fall and rebellion of man." It was inconceivable to him that an upright person could question the divinity of the scriptures or their literal acceptance. As a prayerful man, he led his family in devotions both morning and evening, and pronounced a benediction on every meal. Occasionally he was called upon to pray in public, but they were fumbling, disjointed, albeit genuine prayers. Even in religious affairs he was not given to parsimony, though he was exposed to a great deal of it. He was not an emotional man; he mourned deeply, but his tears were dry; he felt profound gratitude to the divine, but it rarely led to appropriate expression.

He knew that the church, both the society and the building, should be axial to any community, and he had labored for it conscientiously and stubbornly, though the stubbornness permitted him to see the edifice only where it belonged at the north end of Main Street. He was ashamed for himself and for his fellow townsmen that the building had been delayed so long. A commercial center, a courthouse, an academy and a college he had successfully engineered. Town meetings, which were also the meetings of the official church, had been held for a dozen years, but his intercession for a meetinghouse had been unsuccessful. It was still a borrowed building. He had constructed for himself a magnificent new home adjacent to the Courthouse, and his conscience bothered him that there should be a house of Painter, but no house of God.

For years committees had been elected and re-elected to choose sites and stick stakes for the church. The Committee action and the stakes had been disregarded. He had served on more of those committees than anyone else, and he knew the meaning of frustration. And the frustration was mixed with a little resentment, for he had usually not been appointed to a committee until others had confounded the objective and reported failure. In humiliation he had attended church in Daniel Foot's house and in Daniel Foot's barn; he had listened to John Chipman's reading of scripture in Stephen Goodrich's house at the north end of town and in Will Thayer's house at the south end. He had been to baptismal services and prayer meetings in Ebenezer Sumner's barn and had been ousted by Ebenezer with the rest of the congregation when the owner had to fill it with hay. For a time the transient Sunday congregation moved into a tavern and finally into the Courthouse. Even there he felt that God was not being granted the deference due him.

About as much difficulty had been experienced in locating a willing pastor as in locating a suitable place for his pulpit. Many were called but few chose to remain. In 1790 the town had first voted to hire the Reverend Mr. Parmelee "for the term of six months on probation, if the situation of his family was such that they could be removed by sleighing, otherwise for three months." In the end, the provisional terms were not satisfactory to Mr. Parmelee, and sufficient money could not be raised to pay him, because the north-enders would not support him if he preached in the south end of town, and the south-enders would not contribute tithes for sermons delivered in the north end.

After other committees had failed in their bargaining with John Barnett to come for a salary of wheat, Painter took over as Committee Chairman and persuaded the town to offer him fifty pounds a year. Barnett was a candidate for whom it was well worth making sacrifices. He was a Yale graduate of 1780, had preached in New Haven, served as Army Chaplain, and was a favored pupil of Jonathan Edwards. Reverend Barnett came and was ceremoniously ordained in Daniel Foot's barn on November 11, 1790, in the presence of four of the eleven pastors then stationed between Massachusetts and Canada, but he remained for only a few seasons. The churchgoers once more split on the question of where he should preach. When services were moved from Foot's house to Mattock's tavern, the south-enders promptly rebelled and had to be disciplined, excluded or suspended. The resulting civic war made the tenure of any pastor impossible. Mr. Barnett was voted a "dismission" at the end of March 1795.

Again Painter and a supply committee went to work to find a man as gifted at breaking ecclesiastic deadlocks as at delivering a good Sabbath discourse. Thomas Mason was imported from Princeton, Massachusetts, in 1798, to give the Thanksgiving sermon. It was a compelling address on "The Government of God an Occasion of Joy to Mankind." Mason demonstrated that he was an able orator and a reliable theologian; he had more of the poet's touch than most of his contemporaries in the ministry: "The labors and pursuits of the day engage the powers of the mind, and employ the service of our hands, till the dim twilight calls us to suspend our toils, and compose our disordered thoughts. The darksome shades of evening shut from our view the busy scenes of life, and seem to invite us to serious composure and reflection. Secluded from the turbulent and perplexing scenes of worldly pursuits, we seem urged by this retreat to call into view the employments of the past days; carefully to correct the errors into which we have fallen, gratefully to acknowledge the favors we have received from the hand of our maker; earnestly to implore his protection thro the silent watches of the night; his guidance and direction thro the succeeding day; and sincerely to repose our confidence in the uninterrupted course of his governing providence."

He demonstrated that he was well informed in political

172

affairs and did not hesitate to introduce them in the pulpit. From a safe distance the prophet waved an angry fist at Bonaparte: "France, like the ancient Assyrian, may be only the rod of God's anger, and the staff of his indignation to chastise the idolatrous nations around them, and themselves with the rest. For this purpose they may be permitted to take the spoil, and the prey, and to tread them down like the mire of the street. Howbeit, they mean not so, but it is their design to destroy, and cut off nations not a few. Therefore it shall come to pass that, when the Lord hath performed his whole work, he will punish the fruit of the stout heart of the regency of France and the glory of their high looks."

Mason would have been the ideal choice for the Middlebury pastorate. Both the north and the south-enders were satisfied, and Painter used his sober persuasion to get him to remain, but when the candidate uncovered for himself the true state of church affairs, he decided that he wanted no part of them. Mason went back to Massachusetts. A half dozen other candidates came, and reached the same decision Mason had. For more than a decade Middlebury had no regular pastor. On Sundays a portable pulpit was moved to the center of the Courthouse rostrum, and clergymen from neighboring towns, President Atwater, or a College professor gave the morning message.

Painter was a Congregationalist by law as well as by choice, for until 1801 Middlebury was legally Congregational under the provision of the State statute "that when any number of inhabitants of any town or parish, exceeding twenty five, being of a similar sect or denomination of Christians, shall think themselves able to build a meetinghouse for social and public worship . . . such inhabitants shall thereupon be associated

173

and formed into a society . . . and every person of adult age, being a legal voter in such town or parish, shall be considered as being of the religious opinion and sentiment of such society, and liable to be taxed for the purposes aforesaid, unless he shall procure a certificate signed by some minister of the gospel, deacon, elder . . . of the church, congregation, sect or denomination to which he belongs . . . which certificate procured as aforesaid, and recorded at large in the town or parish clerk's office in which he resides, shall exempt him and his property from being taxed for the purposes aforesaid."

Middlebury's legal society was Congregational, and few families from other denominations dared face the social ostracism that went with certification in another church. The law had seen to it that Church and State were securely wedded, and that every man worshiped according to the locally prescribed catechism. But by 1801 so much criticism had been levied against this apparent violation of the Bill of Rights, that the law was relaxed to the extent of permitting a citizen to become exempt from church taxation by filing a simple written declaration with the town clerk: "I do not agree in religious opinion with a majority of the inhabitants of this town."

This breakdown in protection from infringement of other denominations was just the challenge the Congregationalists needed to inspire action on the choice of a site for a church. Even the most ardent members were becoming annoyed and disgruntled. The Methodists and the Episcopalians took courage. Within two months after the alteration of the law, close to fifty members withdrew from "The Religious Society consisting of the Town of Middlebury." Some of the first citizens of the town, Painter's closest friends, like John Chipman and

Daniel Chipman, Horatio Seymour and John Willard, Jonathan Hagar and the College Tutor Joel Doolittle, went over to the Episcopalians even though they had less prospect of building a church in the immediate future than had the Congregationalists.

By December 1801 decision was at last reached to locate the town church on Daniel Chipman's property, several hundred yards north of the Courthouse, and a tax was laid to defray the expense of its erection. But the decision and the tax only served to invite so many to withdraw from the Congregational fold that both had to be revoked. During the next half decade the site for the church was temporarily staked off in a dozen different areas, until Painter finally broke the deadlock at a meeting in 1805 by proposing the old tavern site at the north end of Main Street, where he had always wanted it. He further proposed that the cost be defrayed by the sale of pews rather than by taxation. His plan was the self-evident solution everyone had been awaiting for a generation. He was immediately elected to a committee "to draw a plan of a meetinghouse and expose the pews for sale by public auction, twenty percent to be paid in money, and the remainder in neat cattle or materials for building." His acceptance was protected by a proviso that a reliable pastor be secured to share in shaping plans for a church organization to match the plans for the building, and before that one fruitful meeting ended, the Society had voted to extend the pastoral invitation to a young tutor at the College, Thomas Merrill. Although he had been in Middlebury only a few months, everyone knew and respected him. Mr. Merrill had prepared for the ministry and preferred that calling to teaching. He knew Middlebury and thought he knew what it needed. Within four months the

Tutor became a Pastor and was ordained in the Courthouse.

"Labor faithfully to prepare your flock to rejoice with you in heavenly mansions," exhorted Dr. Asa Burton of Thetford in the ordination charge. "Be clothed with a meek and humble spirit. Be wise as a serpent, and harmless as a dove. Let prayer be your breath. Invite God to aid you in your studies. Pray daily and earnestly for the effusions of the Spirit on this flock; that they may be as a garden well watered, and your labors among them not in vain." Mr. Merrill took good care of his garden. He tilled Middlebury soil with patience and wisdom for nearly forty years, and exchanged counsel with his neighbor Gamaliel Painter almost daily for a decade and a half.

Meantime, the Chairman of the "Committee on Drawing a Plan for the Meeting House and Exposing Pews for Sale" rode down to Bennington to look over the new meetinghouse there and meet its architect, Lavius Fillmore. Fillmore had built several churches in Connecticut and was beginning to be recognized as one of the most skillful designers in New England. The crafty gentleman from Middlebury and the clever architect from Connecticut had a great deal of dexterity in common, and in the end Painter not only persuaded the architect to do the Middlebury church, but also to move his family north. Fillmore was one who could more than match the mechanical ingenuity of his client; he had a sense of artistry and architectural refinement that Painter the Puritan never possessed. He had profited by analysing the structure of the finer churches, the handsome homes and well-built factories of southern New England, and had apparently studied examples or documents of Asher Benjamen, whose manner of embellishment traced itself back to the work of the English Renaissance and Sir

Christopher Wren. To Middlebury he brought both a technique and a taste for aesthetic workmanship. The town needed him. Moreover, he was just the kind of client Painter had been looking for as a purchaser of his mills. To make sure that he had reason for remaining, Painter in a few months expanded the architect's interests to industry and merchandising, and sold him outright both the mills and the water rights at the Falls.

Fillmore had far more grandiose ideas of what Middlebury factories might produce than the former owner had, and while his men were tearing down Painter's recently rebuilt mills to make room for a six-story factory, Fillmore was also overseeing with Painter the construction of one of the most beautiful churches north of Boston. The sale of pews had met with reasonable success, but not enough capital was raised to consider an edifice of stone. It was to be of wood, the largest building in town, seventy-eight feet long and fifty-eight wide, with a steeple over a hundred feet high, commanding the valley as well as Main Street.

But at the height of Painter's exertions for the church, his home was again twice visited by death. To one who lacked the staunch faith and immovable reliance in the Almighty which he possessed, it would appear either that his efforts were being poorly rewarded or that restitution for some secret waywardness were being sought. His second son Joseph died in 1804 after a brief illness, and less than two years later Victoria, still in her middle forties, suddenly left almost empty the big mansion built for her. She had become the most distinguished hostess of the village, sympathetic, convivial and beloved. She had been the stirring motivation to Gamaliel in his struggle to bring cultural and spiritual advantages to the town. A man of less stalwart character would have been broken by the third loss in his family in eight years, but he seemed to accept affliction as part of the course of life. He found explanation but little solace in the sunless creed of his church: "All mankind are the descendants of apostate Adam, and are, by divine constitution, the subjects of total moral depravity; have lost communion with God; are under his wrath and curse; and so made liable to all the miseries of this life . . . God executes his decrees . . . so that all events, however dark and mysterious to mortal view, will infallibly issue in the glory of God and the advancement of his cause."

Tortured by loneliness, but living for his ten-year-old daughter, Abby Victoria, and, to all appearances, unmoved by the double tragedy, he proceeded with plans for the church as though his personal life were in no way associated with his public efforts. Work on the building commenced early in the Spring of 1806 and proceeded in its early stages with such rapidity that the frame was enclosed before autumn. The Legislature was scheduled to meet again in Middlebury that year, and supreme effort was exerted to have the main part of the church ready for their use. The hopes were realized only in part, but on the ninth of October, the august body filed through the piles of lumber on the Commons and found its way under the scaffolding to hear the Election Sermon delivered from the high, unpainted pulpit. The front seats of honor were planks placed across kegs, but the members of the Legislature could survey the fine dimensions of the structure, and most of the townspeople who helped create it.

The man granted the high honor of giving the address was Middlebury's twenty-six year old pastor Merrill. Everyone within commuting distance of the town was there—old and young from the village; the College students en masse; a representative from every town in the State; His Excellency, Isaac Tichenor, Esquire, Governor; His Honor, Paul Brigham, Esquire, Lieutenant Governor; The Honorable Council and The House of Representatives. Mr. Merrill had a message for all of them tucked into his discourse on "Godliness is Profitable for All Things." "The language of eulogy is always too gross for a delicate ear," he eulogized for the benefit of His Excellency. "Let it however be observed, the important posts assigned him, especially his frequent re-election by the suffrages of the people to the first office in the State, more clearly evince the approbation, attachment and respect of the great body of his constituents, than any sentiments which can be expressed in a public discourse . . . So long as he exhibits the character of the faithful and patriotic Governor, a numerous and brave people will have reason to rejoice in his administration and in the great day of account 'to rise up and call him blessed.' "

With sly Yankee understatement and sarcasm he observed that, "Our legislators undoubtedly feel interested for the welfare of the State," and counseled them to be "sensible of the advantages of godliness," "agreeable to the spirit and letter of our constitution," and to keep their deliberations "accountable not to their constituents alone, but to Almighty God, by whom they also must be judged."

Of the College students, whom he had only the year before served as tutor, he commented with feeling, "The impetuous youth from an overfondness of being seen and known, often rushes without reflection upon a world, which is severe to criticise and cold to applaud. From his inexperience, and the precipitancy, which usually attends young genius, he becomes rash and imprudent in his measures, sullies his reputation, and ofttimes, instead of attaining the object of his ambition, sinks into disrepute. Religion checks the ardor and impetuosity of the youth, counsels, cautions, advises and leads him in the path of reputation and usefulness to the goal where he receives those laurels, which will not fade and that crown of glory, which no rival will take from him."

For the benefit of the people, he referred obliquely, but only once, to the building in which he was speaking, a building pungent with fresh pine boards, still littered with shavings and sawdust in the corners, and exposed to the autumn elements. Any personal pride they took in their accomplishment was abruptly removed: "God is the supreme architect," he told them. "This world is a vast building, which He has fitly framed and joined together. Mankind are stewards to whom He assigns the different apartments of this building, to be occupied in their various employments . . . He who stands as the messenger of truth, must declare both to the rich and the poor, the high and the low, the wise and the ignorant, to the most obscure citizen, and to him who wears the robes of magistry, the necessity of the advantages of godliness."

Painter was seated among the legislators. All the challenges, admonitions, and brilliant oratory of Thomas Merrill failed to reduce the·pride and satisfaction he had in the occasion. It was a fitting climax of his career as town father. His only regret was that Victoria and his two sons could not be there to share it with him.

The note of triumph in the occasion, however, was somewhat premature. The citizens had all but exhausted themselves in their effort to prepare the church for the occasion, and the public commendation was enough to last for a long time. They suddenly relaxed in their zeal to see the building completed.

It was three years before the last coat of paint was applied to the steeple and cornices, before the last of the interior scaffolding was down, and the pews were installed. Painter repeatedly had to return to the members of the congregation with appeals for further aid. He needed a warehouse in which to keep the contributions, for they were mostly in lumber, nails, grain, plaster, cement, cows, shingles, and stone—or labor, drayage, and craftsmanship. But visible progress on the building, as well as the legislative commendation, and the presence of an ordained pastor had a remarkable effect on the membership of the church. Many of those who had withdrawn pleaded for the privilege of being readmitted. They were taken back, in accordance with the Articles of Consociation: "Should visible fruits of repentance at any time appear, even the excommunicated are to be cordially returned." In less than two years, more than a hundred members were added.

The dedication which was at last scheduled for May 31, 1809, was sublimely austere, but dignified and grand. The pastor of the church remained humbly in the background, giving only a few introductory remarks and reading the scripture. The Reverend Mr. Tullar of Royalton made the dedicatory prayer, and the distinguished clergyman, Heman Hall, of Rutland, presented the principal discourse from the duplex text, "And she gave the savory food and the bread, which she had prepared, into the hand of his son, Jacob." A great choir, which had practiced for weeks, sang *a capella*, and the whole congregation joined in the ode which Samuel Swift had composed for the occasion:

> Almighty Father, Son
> And Spirit, triune God!
> This temple consecrate

And make it thine abode;
We dedicate
This House to Thee
And let it be
A Heav'nly Gate.

It was the temple rather than any of the dignitaries present, or the addresses, the odes, the anthems or the prayers that created the occasion. The people were awed by the sheer beauty of the building, its exquisite detail and majestic dimensions. The massive white facade and the handsome spire rising one-hundred-thirty-five feet at the end of Main Street, where Deming's unsightly tavern had stood, gave an entirely new accent, and a new focal point, to the village. And the interior with the high central pulpit, the circular pews, groined arches, simple Ionic columns, distinctive capitals and graceful gallery, bathed in a luxury of white, was an anthem and a prayer in itself.

Gamaliel Painter's vision of a church had materialized.

10 LEGISLATOR

Lawmaking in early Vermont was a carefree occupation, approached with a practical sense of humor, an inordinate amount of horseplay and at least an affectation of sincerity when political convictions were under attack. There was little pretension about lawmakers; they were servants of the people, appointed to perform a serious job, but among themselves they were themselves, Green Mountain Boys with graying hair over the temples and less agility in their movements than they had demonstrated in pre-Revolutionary forays.

Painter's was a slow sense of humor, but on the way to Rutland for his first Assembly meeting he was alerted to the caprice of his fellow legislators. Customarily the Assemblyman from the more distant towns left home several days before the session was due to start, called for other members en route, spent a few convivial nights at hospitable taverns, and, in a state of controlled insobriety gradually converged on the temporary capital en masse. Including Governor Chittenden and legislative followers, the body had swelled to a considerable number by the time they picked up Gamaliel in the fall of 1786 and proceeded to Salisbury where a festive banquet was being prepared at Sawyer's Public House.

To provide a suitable welcome for the party, the Salisbury pranksters had secured a swivel left over from Revolutionary days, hidden it in the brush close to the tavern, and loaded it heavily. It was touched off at the moment when the Governor and the Assemblymen were dismounting. No company could have been caught more unprepared for the deafening salute. Horses reared and galloped off; Painter and other legislators swinging off their saddles were thrown to the ground; the Governor, caught with one foot in a stirrup, was hurled horizontal; and the entire company was left awkwardly strewn over the Inn yard, momentarily stunned and mute as if the cannon had been fired into their midst rather than as a salute of welcome. But over Sawyer's bar they soon recovered what composure was necessary, and passed off the hearty welcome as a fitting overture to the session of 1786.

The first laws of Vermont were not composed by amateurs; for the most part they were lifted from the statutes of Connecticut, with the apologetic addition that, "Whereas, it is impossible at once to provide particular statutes adapted to all cases wherein law may be necessary . . . so much of the common law of England, as is not repugnant to the Constitution . . . shall be, and continue to be, law within this State."

184

During the early days of the settlements there was anarchy. "The truth is," commented Daniel Chipman, who knew from firsthand experience how ungovernable some of his compatriots were, "there was no regular government in the State. Everything was unsettled; no social compact existed, nor any bond of Union, save that which resulted from common wants and common dangers; and everything that bore the semblance of organization, was the premature offspring of urgent necessity."

This was the commonwealth that Gamaliel Painter first knew. Step by step he saw the primeval disorder change to civil order, and he had a personal part in most of the development. He was a member of the Dorset Convention in 1775, when the declaration of Vermont independence was first considered, a member of the Windsor Convention in 1777 when the State Constitution was adopted, and a member of the Legislature when later editions of the laws of Vermont were being propagated. For over twenty-five years after the Revolution he was intermittently associated with lawmaking as a member of the Assembly or the Governor's Council. He was more often a back-seat legislator than an Assembly spokesman, but his ponderous wisdom found its way into the journals and statutes during the entire formative period of the State.

The Constitution, as Painter helped set it up, edit, and amend it, called for a Governor, a Lieutenant Governor, a Council of twelve, a General Assembly consisting of a representative from each town, and a Council of Censors, whose duty it was once every seven years to compose a critique on state legislation. The unicameral House met once or twice a year, and supreme legislative power rested with it. Assemblymen considered anything from constitutional amendments to

185

Alexander Twidmire's petition for financial backing in setting up his foundry. As a body it was highly conservative and slow to adopt any change involving ideology. The Constitution gave the people their inalienable rights; the Assembly protected them. And just in case the Legislature made too hurried a decision in session excitement, the Governor's Council could reflect on the issues at leisure and point out the error of their ways. Then the Council of Censors, surveying the march of events from long range could criticize the Governor's Council, the Assembly, the Governor or any trend that failed to move in the proper democratic direction. The principle behind the process was to keep inviolate Section I, Chapter I, of the Constitution: "That all men are born equally free and independent, and have certain natural, inherent and inalienable rights, amongst which are the enjoying and defending of life and liberty; acquiring, possessing and protecting property, and pursuing and obtaining happiness and safety." No male over twenty-one and no female under eighteen could be "holden by law to serve any person as a servant, slave, or apprentice," unless by their own consent, or when "bound by law for the payment of debts, damages, fines, costs, and the like." Minors did not matter; it was a presbyterial world. The checks and double checks on Authority were to preserve what Vermonters had battled with Great Britain to acquire. Painter, like every other freeman who had helped settle that argument and had helped establish a new nation and a new state, wanted to be doubly sure that there could be no abridgment of individual rights.

For that reason, the Governor was given a title, but singularly little power to go with it. He was nebulously directed "to take care that the laws be faithfully executed," but he could not even appoint a commisson except by consent of a quorum of Council members. He was Captain-General and Commander-in-Chief of the State Army, but he was prohibited from taking personal command until so instructed by his Council. He annually delivered a message to the Assembly, but the message contained no demands and few recommendations that any minister of the gospel could not have given as appropriately. About the only appointive power he had was the designation of his own Secretary, and that power was granted by constitutional revision. And, lest he conceive of this position as anything but that of a servant to the people, he was given a servant's salary. As late as 1801, when a bill was presented proposing that his compensation be increased to $700 a year, it was overwhelmingly voted down. Painter was in the Assembly to contribute his negative ballot. Someone, convinced that the salary was not commensurate with the dignity, if not the responsibilities, of the office, ventured another resolution, "inquiring into the salary paid to the Governor of this State." Painter, like a majority of his fellow assemblymen, resoundingly voted down even making an inquiry. The Governor needed a new coat, and before the session closed, an incautious friend introduced from the floor still another bill recommending $800. The nays and Painter won. In one last effort, after the condition of the Governor's tailoring had been duly aired, $750 was mentioned, and the wearied Assembly changed its mind. By a vote of 92 to 79 they gave him the raise, though Painter voted to the last in the negative. No additional powers went with the additional salary.

The Governor had to share practically all of the executive authority with his Council, the members of which were elected by the same procedure he was; each freeman named twelve candidates, and the twelve in the State having the highest nomination were declared elected. They met with the General Assembly and between sessions whenever the Governor had business to transact. As a body, they could commission or appoint officers, temporarily fill vacancies occasioned by emergencies or death, "prepare such business as may appear to them necessary to lay before the General Assembly;" they sat as judges to consider impeachment cases, had limited power of pardon and reprieve, could lay embargoes or, for a period of thirty days, prohibit exportation of any commodity; they granted licenses, and they could call special sessions of the Legislature. Every Council member automatically became a Justice of the Peace upon election, by virtue of his office. In practice, Vermont had thirteen co-governors, and Painter twice served as one of them.

When the Governor made his address it usually contained the collective expression of the Council:

> The enacting of laws should ever be a business of mature deliberation. The happiness and safety of society does not depend on the multiplicity of its laws. Laws should be few in number, explicit, and duly enforced. What the operation of a law will be upon a community, the most discerning cannot foretell. The partial evil is sometimes noticed upon the promulgation of a law, which is often greatly overbalanced by its more general and beneficial effects. The only sure mode of deciding upon the merits of a statute, is to submit to the process of patient experiment. Hence it follows that legislatures should be as careful in repealing as in enacting laws. Among the public acts passed by the last General Assembly, it is believed that the act relating to insolvent debtors is not sufficiently explicit and guarded, to secure the rights of creditors, and afford the remedy intended for debtors. An investigation, by the Assembly possessing accurate knowledge

of the operation of this statute, and some others recently enacted, will determine if amendments are necessary . . . In order to make sanguinary punishments less necessary it is strongly recommended, that means should be provided for punishing by hard labor, those who should be convicted of crimes not capital . . . The weakness of our county gaols throughout the State, the frequent escape of persons confined for crimes . . . impress it upon me as a duty, to draw the attention of the Legislature to the erecting of a state prison . . . The public business will always be transacted to the greatest advantage, when it is done in the exercise of wisdom, of candor, and of moderation.

The conciliatory tone of the Governor's observations, and the assumption that the observations had the endorsement of his twelve disciples, was conducive to responsive action. On the very afternoon that Isaac Tichenor suggested investigation, Painter was named on a Committee "to examine and report what measures are necessary to be taken for punishing by hard labor those who shall be convicted of crimes not capital." The governor's moderate manner was effective.

The Council of Censors, elected every seventh year, addressed the Legislature with equal deference and moderation. It was a deliberative unit of thirteen, neither executive nor legislative; though they had the posture of a high legislative court. It was their duty "to inquire, whether the constitution has been preserved inviolate in every part, during the last septenary; and whether the legislative and executive branches of government have performed their duty as guardians of the people." They were instructed to "inquire whether the public taxes have been justly laid and collected," how state funds had been spent, whether laws had been properly executed. They had power to subpoena persons, to pass public censures, order

189

impeachments and recommend the repealing of laws. The full powers were seldom employed. They were the critics of the critics, but the criticism was usually more laudatory than reproachful: "This Council, in examining the proceedings of the Legislature and Executive Departments of this Government, during the last Septenary, are happy to find no proceedings which we judge unconstitutional . . . It gives us great pleasure, when we take a retrospective view of the multiplicity of the intricacies of business, that is brought before the Legislature, that there are so few instances where they have erred; and are happy to find that wisdom and stability mark the proceedings of our public bodies; and that this government is daily gaining knowledge and respectability."

The censors had a tendency to present their criticism so politely, so graciously and in terms of such generality that they offended few and inspired no world-shaking action, but 1813 suddenly saw a new order. The Censors, that year, stepped into their role with spirit and, in pages of obloquy, blasted the previous legislature for passing an act "suspending the civil process against the persons and property of the officers and soldiers of the State while in service." On seven counts they labeled it a violation of the Constitution of the United States and concluded that "not to remonstrate would be to join in overthrowing the liberties of our country, and betraying a trust reposed in us by the constitution of this State. Resolved, that this council do earnestly recommend to the legislature . . . the immediate and unqualified repeal of said act . . ." The Legislature went to work.

But the Council of Censors had no authority other than to recommend. They could make no binding declaration regarding constitutionality. All practical authority rested with the

Assembly, which was concerned with the people and the everyday problems of the people—as much concerned with maintaining the poor, keeping nuisances off the highway, making the Sabbath day holy, and destroying thistles, wolves, and panthers, as in capital punishment, high finance and the civil process. The Legislature was interested in morals and personal integrity, as well as material benefits. Painter lived in an era of fence-making and road building, when the first fences and the first roads in a new country were being laid, and the laws had to be made by men and for men who were trying to define boundaries, trying to draw reasonable restriction while promoting expansion and communication. Elemental laws had to be made against polygamy and adultery, against drunkenness and cursing, against counterfeiting and lying. Constructive statutes had to be written to promote the chartering of toll bridges and ferries, to designate what bills of credit and money would be acceptable currency, to regulate trials and appeals, pleas and pleadings. New institutions had to be encouraged, but regulated; new offices created, but their powers defined; commerce had to be sponsored, but restricted. Vermont law began at the beginning. After the first constitution was adopted the miscellany of statutes were added year by year as it became necessary to cope with new situations, or as some town representative became convinced that a law was better than an understanding. The Assembly, with one representative from each town, carried the full responsibility for promoting the best interests of the State.

The lawmakers were as heterogeneous as a jury: crafty attorneys, honest but slow-witted farmers, merchants, amateur mechanics. Gathered in the Courthouse or Town Hall of Windsor, Vergennes, Rutland, Castleton, with their hats and greatcoats on against the autumn chill, they were anything but prepossessing in appearance, and Painter fitted well into his environment. Their attempts to be formal or dignified were not reassuring. All were required to remove their headgear in the presence of the Governor or members of the Council, or when addressing the speaker, unless one could certify that he was a Quaker. A Friend was authorized to follow his conscience in the matter. There were fluent speakers and dull, awkward speakers. An officer of the House who failed to be punctual in his attendance was promptly "reduced to private station," and any member who was habitually tardy or absent was expelled. The rules of order prescribed that fellow members be addressed as "Mr."; they were so addressed, but the tone of voice often reflected something beside respect. A member voting in the minority was forbidden from calling for reconsideration of a measure; when yeas and nays were demanded, every member present had to vote or give adequate excuse to the House for not voting; no business of any sort could be conducted in the presence of the Governor or a member of his Council, except items which they brought to it; no act could be voted on until it had rested for at least twenty-four hours; no member could be on more than three committees at a time. Galleries—when there were galleries— were open to spectators, but the House Messenger stood on guard at the door to prevent entrance to the floor of any visitor short of a Senator of the United States, a Member of Congress or a Judge of the Supreme Court. Each Assembly made its own rules of procedure, but they varied little from year to year.

According to the Constitution, the Assembly was composed of the persons "most noted for wisdom and virtue," and

192

the same constitution authorized them to prepare bills and enact them into laws, judge the authority of elections, redress grievance, impeach state criminals, grant charters of incorporation, constitute towns and counties, choose delegates to Congress, elect judges, sheriffs, justices, major generals and brigadier generals, and in general assume all "powers necessary for the legislation of a free and sovereign state."

During the fourteen intermittent years that Painter served on the Assembly between 1786 and 1810 he played a part in all of these functions. He was an acceptable committee member for any cause and usually held its limit of three at one time. His background in surveying and road building made him a valuable addition to a committee facing precarious problems of changing town and county boundaries, or approving new roads. His experience in business brought him membership on Assembly committees to consider "provisions for supplying the treasury," and to nominate committees "to superintend the expenditures of monies raised by land taxes." His judgeship qualified him for committee investigations of individual grievances and alleged injustice. As early as 1791 he was one of the seven given the responsibility of weighing "the expediency of opening a communication between the waters of Lake Champlain and Hudson's River; and also of rendering the navigation of Connecticut River more easy and advantageous." And twelve years later, when the question of promoting a state bank at Windsor was a major item on the legislative agenda, Painter was one of the five Assembly financiers asked to make recommendations. The issue carried through the entire session of 1803, and on November second was finally approved by a narrow majority. But as a result he had to suffer the indignity of being called to task by the Council, who reported their nonconcurrence in one of the strongest criticisms ever ventured by that body:

> . . . Bank bills cannot be made a legal tender, must prove a calamity to the citizens in general, and especially to those who dwell at a distance from the proposed banks . . . The tendency of banks would be to palsy the vigor of industry, and to stupefy the vigilance of economy . . . Banks would tend to divert the attention of the speculator, the inexperienced youth, the indolent and the incautious, from those honest, honorable and sure sources of mediocrity and independence . . . Banks by facilitating enterprises both hazardous and unjustifiable, are natural sources of all that class of vices which arise from the gambling system, and which cannot fail to act as sure and fatal, though slow, poisons to the republic . . . Banks tend strongly to draw off the dependence of debtors from their own exertions . . . , have a violent tendency, in their natural operation, to draw into the hands of the few a large proportion of the property at present fortunately diffused among the many . . . , would credit none but persons of affluence . . . , and enable those who have credit with them to loan money at an exorbitant interest . . . By the establishment of banks, government could, in our opinion, go farther than could have been contemplated in its original institution. Government, we apprehend, was not designed to open fields of speculation . . . ; much less was it designed as a means of drawing property out of the hands of the less wealthy, to place it in the hands of the more wealthy.

The Governor and Council that year did not approve of State banks. Painter did. And Windsor eventually got its bank.

By Assembly regulation, Committees were not permitted to sit during the hours when the Legislature was in session. Painter's membership on so many of them meant that most of his evenings and early morning hours during October and November were taken up with extra-session duties. On occa-

194

sion, he had the chore of helping to arrange the agenda for the whole session, the thankless task of receiving, sorting and counting the thousands of public votes for the Governor, Lieutenant Governor, Counsellors and Treasurer, and the challenging job of helping "to devise some means for settling disputes concerning town lines and taxes on Gores."

For a man as active in the Legislature as he was, he introduced very few bills, and these related entirely to business ventures in which he was involved or to matters of taxation, roads, or institutions from his home town or county. Most of these were bills which he presented at the request of his constituents, but all too frequently he lacked the necessary oratory to see them through, and helplessly accepted the privilege of withdrawing a petition or letting it lie on the table.

His impartial convictions as well as his prejudices were often obvious in the drawl of his *yea* or *nay* when a record of the vote was demanded. He voted against extending the lines of Addison County to the Onion River. He voted against any additional financial provision for "transient, idle, impotent and poor persons." He voted against the division of Windsor into half shires, was in the minority and had the satisfaction of seeing the bill repealed the following year. He voted for the incorporation of the Vermont Manufacturing Society, but he was again in the minority. He favored a more permanent home for the Legislature, even when Middlebury was not being considered as a possibility for the Capitol. He was naturally against the bill, in 1801, which permitted a person to withdraw his support of the legal community church by merely presenting a written "decent" to the Town Clerk. And when the Legislature was forced to consider having individual *yeas* and *nays* publicized, he voted for anonymity,

195

though the consciences of so many others bothered them that he was on the losing side. His own personal experience was reflected in his casting a ballot against a bill making it unconstitutional for judges of courts and justices of the peace to hold a seat in the Legislature, but he lost. He favored strong state forces and voted for an appropriation to purchase brass ordnance in 1803; too many others, however, considered it an unwarranted expenditure. He wanted to restrict hawkers and peddlers by requiring them to secure licenses. He consistently voted for any new proposed turnpikes.

When issues arose which were personal to him he frequently managed to abstain from voting or was conveniently excused from the floor on urgent business, which he somehow managed to keep up even while serving the State. He was not present to commit himself on matters dealing with Ethan Allen; his vote was not recorded when his friend, Colonel Lyon of Orwell, was seeking a loan of eight hundred pounds from the State to repair a blast furnace and "put it in blast" in competition with one projected for Middlebury; he preferred to be noncommittal on the petition of Stephen Keys, "stating that in consequence of the rapid depreciation of paper money, losses in navigation, sickness and other misfortunes, he had become invalid; and praying for an act of insolvency."

By 1813, when Painter was first elected to the Governor's Council, he had seen enough experience in the Assembly to be considered one of the leading politicians in the State. Political parties had also matured and Painter was a recognized figure among the Vermont Federalists. The idea of a conquest of Canada had become a political issue, bringing possible war into the front dooryard of the State. "War" and "Peace" parties had fought such strenuous campaigns the previous summer that the Governor felt compelled to re-monstrate against political corruption, referring to "those local and party views which stimulate one part of the community to trample on the rights of the other, and to sport with the feelings and happiness of their fellow men." The Council, labeling themselves, "the watchmen upon the walls of the political safety and happiness of the people," had chorused their deep concern for the "multiplied aggressions of the military power . . . upon the civil rights, privileges, and property of the peaceable, unoffending and defenceless citizens of this state."

The Assembly and Council met in 1813 admittedly "under prospects not of the most flattering." "Our political horizon," acknowledged one spokesman, "is encircled with clouds somewhat pretentious. It is a period . . . most eventful in the history of the world: a crisis demanding the united wisdom, prudence and firmness of the whole community." The tension mounted at the very opening of the Assembly when the Governor's right to assume office was contested due to an alleged miscount of ballots, but Martin Chittenden's embarrassment was minor in comparison with Painter's.

On Election Day the previous September, when it appeared that the town of Colchester, a few miles north of Burlington, might not go War Party, a politically zealous Major had been persuaded to round up a detachment of some two hundred officers and men and march them double file to the polls of William Munson's house in Colchester. There they had been plied with gallons of rum, supplied with the proper ballots and commanded to exercise their right of suffrage. Under a certain amount of duress the Town Clerk had administered to them as a group the necessary oaths, and obediently neglected to record their names. The military ballots were enough to stuff the box in favor of the Major's party. And the election returns were so close that the Colchester vote carried the election against Painter. His opponent claimed 16,957, Painter received 16,755. However, the Assembly Committee on the counting of ballots had caught wind of the connivance, discarded the Colchester vote, and declared Painter elected. His welcome to Montpelier was a resolution that the Colchester ballots were not illegal and a petition that his seat be vacated to allow the lawfully elected incumbent to occupy it. Painter kept his seat. It took an investigating committee most of the session to smoke out all the facts of the case, but in the end there was no question of his right to the high office. Every officer of the State knew the Councilor from Middlebury and his *cause célèbre* by the middle of November.

Since the early days of the Constitution, the voice of the Council had gradually increased in importance until the Council was virtually a second House, was frequently referred to as such, and was consulted on all important bills; Assembly committees were merely instructed "to join from Council." During the session of 1813 Painter moved from one committee room to another, assessing the affairs of state, criticizing, reviewing, investigating, reporting. Decisions had to be reached on "the mode for detaching the militia"; "examining the several acts relating to sheriffs, high bailiffs, their bondsmen and sureties"; appointment of "Thursday, the second day of December next as a day of public Thanksgiving"; measures to be taken "to perpetuate in its purity the merino breed of sheep"; removal of the banks at Middlebury and Burlington to Woodstock, and burning all the bills of the Vermont Bank (The Middlebury bank had been robbed and the integrity of its of-

198

ficers was in question); inquiry into the "cause why the town of Canaan have not paid their taxes"; inquiry into the safety of county gaol yards; examining "the situation of the treasury of this state" and determining "what taxes it will be necessary to lay for the support of government for the year ensuing"; "the expediency of passing a law making it the duty of each landowner in this state to review the bounds of his land within certain limited times"; "electing visitors of the state prison for the year ensuing"; electing two brigadier generals; "an act to prevent intercourse with the enemies of this and the United States." And, lest the complications of Painter's election be repeated, the Council itself addressed to the Assembly a resolution calling for a committee to devise suitable rules by which future canvassing committees shall be governed in receiving, sorting, and counting votes for . . . councillors."

Painter took his Council office for the second year in 1814 without any questions being raised. In fact, on the opening day of the Assembly he was appointed chairman of the Council, and on the following day Chairman of both the Council and the Assembly in joint Committee. The session was much less stormy than the one of the previous year; the legislators were too busy congratulating themselves on the way the war had turned on the Canadian border to indulge in party politics. Each wanted to outdo the other in singing the praises of their gallant forces. "On the subject of the victory achieved by Commodore Macdonough and his associates, on Lake Champlain, the feelings of this assembly are inexpressible," wrote one member in an official communiqué to the Governor. "The great inequality of force, the sanguinary nature of the contest, the instances of individual heroism, and, above all, the immense importance of the result to the people of this State,

leave no room but for emotions of wonder and gratitude."
The victory transcended politics.

Painter was kept busy attending Committee meetings, but there was optimism now instead of the languid pessimism of 1813. And more thought could be devoted to civil affairs than military. He had brought a petition to the Legislature calling for financial aid to Middlebury College and was in a top position to see that it was not overlooked. The financial straits of the broken State Bank at Middlebury were also under warm discussion, and in canny Yankee reasoning he associated the two to create a solution for both. Reference was repeatedly made in the Assembly to the College petition. And Painter saw to it that the Committee was well grounded on facts. At length, on the fourteenth anniversary of the chartering of the College, the Committee returned its recommendation to the General Assembly:

> Your Committee to whom was referred the petition of the President and Fellows of Middlebury College, unanimously report that they are fully impressed . . . That the growth of Middlebury College has been unexampled in our country—that the exertions of individuals for its promotion have been great, and attended with signal success—that the institution has obtained a reputation, which . . . renders it an ornament to the State, and that it is highly deserving of public patronage—that your committee, believing it to be the disposition of the legislature to aid an institution which has done so much to promote the cause of education and virtue in the State, have turned their attention to the means by which the legislature might exercise their munificence—that in the opinion of your committee, the property and concerns of the State bank which (owing to the embarrased state of those concerns, and the care and expense of agency . . .) would not be of great value to the state, might in the hands of the corporation of Middlebury College, essentially aid the insti-

tution under their charge, increase its usefulness, and in that way be applied to the lasting benefit and honor of the state— therefore your committee recommend that the property of said bank . . . be granted and transferred to the President and Fellows of Middlebury College, subject to the following conditions, viz. that said President and Fellows be obliged to pay all the outstanding notes, bills and checks of said bank— that the lands derived to the state, by means of said bank, be, and remain, a permanent fund to said college . . .

The College was in a bad financial plight. President Atwater had just resigned, and the salary of the new president had to be raised to $700.00; the trustees had been forced to increase upperclass tuition to $4.50 a term and up the rent of rooms to seventy-five cents a term. The College was not making ends meet. Taking over the assets of the Bank might help, but there was tremendous risk in assuming the liabilities.

The recommendation was tabled from day to day, referred from committee to committee and just before the session ended was referred to the next session. Painter was convinced that the next session would not be as munificent, and, considering the terms of the bequest, he doubted that he or other college trustees could afford to be interested anyway. He acknowledged defeat.

In this defeat he ended his career as a Vermont statesman. He had risen from town moderator to a position on the Council close to that of the Governor. He returned to private life in 1815. Politics had never been easy for him, but by sheer force of character and determination he had won a place in the political annals of Vermont.

11 CIVIL ENGINEER

The Surveyor of Highways was an authoritarian covertly detested and openly respected in every Vermont town. With him rested the responsibility for keeping the roads passable in summer and broken out in winter; and for those two purposes every able-bodied male between twenty-one and sixty, except ministers, schoolmasters, college students and professors, was at his command. His whim could draft fifty farmers from the corn field or the corner store to clear a stretch of road across which a summer blow had leveled a tangle of trees. In the first good days for spring plowing, he could interrupt with a summons to fill the ruts in a mile of swamp road where the bottom had dropped out; in sub-zero February he could demand that they leave their hearth fires to attack the mountainous drifts on the road to Salisbury. From the Surveyor of Highways there was no recourse—except through the Courts. His orders carried the authority of an army colonel or the village sheriff, and they were backed by the full weight of State law with fines which few could afford.

The law exacted each year a minimum tax of four days for the purpose of making and repairing highways at seventy-five cents per day if the work were done between the first of May and the first of July, fifty-five if it were between September and November. Winter work was gratuitous. In practice this meant that the eligible were compelled to put in four summer days of hard labor with no pay, or subsidize someone else at the rate of seventy-five or fifty-five cents, depending on the season. The law required the Surveyor to give three days notice of recruitment, but the caprice of Vermont weather did not work in favor of the law. The days of grace were usually suspended, for ruts, ripe for working, could freeze overnight; snow drifts accumulated without advance warning; and a spring freshet could carry out a bridge in an hour. Men had to work on the road when the work had to be done. The tax of four days was a bare minimum and did not often settle one's obligation. Emergency snow breaking, construction of new roads, repairing of washouts, and bridge work could extend the forced labor into a full week, two weeks or longer. And for a modicum of fifty cents, a pair of oxen with team and tools could be commandeered along with the man power, though the town provided ox-shovels, plows and scrapers. Each man furnished his own shovel, rake or hoe, custom-built by the local smith. The total responsibility for mustering men, assembling equipment, and getting the road in shape rested with the district Surveyor of Highways. Painter was the man.

204

CIVIL ENGINEER

As an artificer during the Revolution, Gamaliel had helped build every type of necessity from forts and bridges to smithy shops and polite quarters for the general. When he had been without the proper equipment and materials he had been obliged to improvise. When there was need for haste he had learned to get the most out of his men in the shortest possible time. Surveying highways offered small challenge to the civil engineer who had served as Captain of the Artificers, but he was ready to contribute his wealth of experience to lesser ventures. He knew his men, he knew the soil, and he knew the lay of every last ledge, swamp and hillside in the county from surveying hundreds of pitches. He had laid out many of the roads connecting the settlements, and he had an active common sense to dictate how a road should be planned to avoid the steepest grades, the bottomless lands and ornery landowners. His interest in road building went back to his first arrival in the Green Mountain wilderness. At that time the grants were cut only by a few unkept military highways, by Indian trails and the swathes through the forest made by settlers like himself. Roads stopped where a navigable stream coursed in the right direction, and thanks to Otter Creek, the Lake, and the Connecticut River, road building was delayed for decades. Long after Middlebury had become a respectable settlement, there was still no highway to the outside world. New settlers slashed a way through the woods for their oxcarts; old settlers preferred their home-made scows and canoes for shopping trips, churchgoing and social visits. Otter Creek and Lake Champlain remained the thoroughfares of trade, and Lover's Lane, following the meanders of the Creek on the east bank from the site of Painter's original cabin to the Falls, was for years the best apology of a roadway in the region.

But as Middlebury grew, and as towns in the vicinity grew,

the people were afflicted with a kind of claustrophobia. There was suddenly a desperation to find easy and quick access to the outside, whether they expected to use that access or not. Everyone became imbued with the idea of building roads at any cost, town roads, county roads, post roads, market roads, turnpikes. For a brief time there was more enthusiasm for communication than cultivation, more interest in extending roads than in extending fields and pastures. The Surveyor of Highways had his heyday.

An application for a new highway, signed by three freeholders and addressed to the selectmen made it mandatory for them to construct one or explain to a court why it was not possible. And when the application cut across town lines it went to the Legislature:

> It is hereby enacted by the General Assembly of the State of Vermont, that Gamaliel Painter of Middlebury, Theophilus Harrington of Clarendon, and Stephen Williams of Rutland, be, and they are hereby appointed, a committee to lay out and survey, . . . a road to lead from Middlebury Falls in the County of Addison, through the towns of Cornwall, Whiting, Sudbury, Hubbardton, Castleton and Poultney to the northeastern part of the town of Granville, in the State of New York, there to unite with the turnpike road leading from said Granville to Troy, in the said State of New York. And the said Committee are hereby directed to lay out and survey the said road, in such manner as they shall judge will, in the greatest degree, accommodate the public, in passing from the said Middlebury Falls to Troy aforesaid . . .

In such an appointment, the Legislature was merely recognizing the necessity of a road from Middlebury to Troy, New York. After the completion of the survey, the towns through which the projected highway passed might be persuaded to divide the cost. New roads could be built by applying the annual four-day tax, with such additions as the town might vote, or a land tax of one, two or three cents on every privately owned acre in the town might be authorized by the Legislature. And there was always the possibility of a ground lottery. Lotteries were immoral and illegal until they were endorsed by the Assembly, but they were recommended orthodox procedure for causes of public interest; Painter had even sponsored one for the reconstruction of the bridge across the Falls. And if lotteries, land tax and road tax were voted out, chances were good that private capital would be available for a turnpike. The road had to go through. The public demanded it.

Through the Surveyor of Highways, the State gave to the towns a fairly free hand on road construction and operation, but it was solicitous of the landowner when individual justice was concerned. If an owner raised valid objections to having a road bisect his barnyard, the best lawyers and the highest local court went into action. But usually the property owner was more than cooperative, even though it meant building new four-and-a-half-foot fences along either side of the right of way to keep his swine and cattle confined. A road was his lifeline, and state law protected him against any injustice in maintenance of that life line. Culpable selectmen who delayed opening a road that had been legally ordered were personally subject to fines of five dollars for every month of delay. The State held the big stick and kept it poised. And a whole town could be fined for neglect in the upkeep of a through highway: "Every town in this state through which a county or market road is or may be laid, shall be liable to be fined for neglecting to keep in repair such county or market highways and bridges in such town, on indictment found by the grand jurors . . ." Moreover, the town could be sued on the just complaint of any private transient who felt that he or his property had been damaged in transit over a town-supported road: "If any special damage shall happen to any person or persons, or to his, her or their teams or carriages, by means of any insufficiency or want of repairs of any highway or public bridges, in any town within this state; the party sustaining such damage shall have right to recover the same in an action on the case, against such town." It behooved the towns not to disregard their obligations.

The only phase of road building on which the State law was silent was its quality. A width of not less than three rods was prescribed, but what existed between the borders of that three rods, what its gradient should be, what the foundation, the drainage, and the surface were, concerned only the town, and was left to local discretion. Discretion often faltered. A road up to the hubs in mud was passable. Boulders and stumps over which any ordinary high-slung chaise could pass were not ruled out. Outcroppings of reasonably smooth ledge were sought rather than avoided. Fords across less precarious streams and swamps were marked, but no effort was made to bridge them. Conveyances were built of the stoutest oak and walnut, with wheel rims or felloes up to twelve inches in width, to withstand the tortuous roadbeds, the boulders and tree stumps. And on the less traveled roads, driving visibility was low because of the high grass, weeds and brush growing luxuriantly between the ruts. There were periods in the spring after the frost had gone out when everyone but the most venturesome stayed home, and periods in midsummer, after the road had been scythed, when actual pleasure might be found in driving a carriage cautiously over the hard clay. In winter the snow in the highway was rolled and packed; in summer the roadways were trimmed and harrowed, but even with these precautions, passing another vehicle called for determination, skill and calculated risk.

The jurisdiction of the Surveyor of Highways extended only to the public roads, and year by year the extent of his responsibilities decreased as private turnpikes took their place. The fervor for roads knew no bounds, and private taxation for roads had been strained to the limit. Turnpikes were the answer, and by the early 1800's there were probably more turnpike companies in the State than any other one kind of corporation. In 1805 alone fifteen new companies were chartered by the Assembly. In their excitement to have a highway out of the woods, the public, without giving much thought to what they were doing, abruptly began relinquishing to private investment their primary utility. The key highways were no longer theirs. Every free road was interrupted by the inevitable toll gate where a substantial fee was demanded of each passenger before a vehicle could proceed.

Painter fell in line with the times. He gave up his job as Surveyor of Highways and went into the turnpike business. Over a period of fifteen years he had an investment as well as a hand in engineering most of the turnpikes in the vicinity of Middlebury, but his biggest venture was with the Bread Loaf road through Ripton Gap. In 1800, the nearest reliable road over the Green Mountains was by way of Rutland, thirty-five miles south. The Bread Loaf road was little more than a trail and rambling cart path impossible for a coach or carriage. It meant a detour of nearly a hundred miles to reach a town like Hancock scarcely more than ten distant. Painter helped make the short cut. In answer to his petition, the Assembly conceded that, "Whereas the public road leading from the Courthouse in Middlebury . . . to the Courthouse in Windsor . . . is circuitous, mountainous and rocky, and the expense of shortening, making and repairing a road, over said ground, would be much greater than ought to be borne by the Towns through which the same may pass, the petitioners should be extended the privilege of locating a proper thoroughfare."

There was an original corporation of thirteen members, including personal friends of Painter like Daniel Chipman, Samuel Miller, Seth Storrs and Samuel Mattocks. To them, their associates, successors, heirs and assigns was granted a charter for the Center Turnpike Company with the understanding that they "shall have and enjoy all the privileges which are incident to corporations, for the purpose of laying out, making, keeping in repair, and improving a turnpike road, from the Courthouse in Middlebury, in the County of Addison, to Woodstock."

They were authorized to lay out a road through "any lands where it shall be found convenient," and to alter it as they saw fit "best to accommodate the public and promote the general object and design of the corporation." They were required to make the road four rods wide and the "path for travel" at least eighteen feet wide. No allowance had to be made to owners for any land taken by the road if it had not been improved or enclosed, nor for any sites of old roads, but if property owners chose to dispute the purchase price offered for their land, they could discuss it with the Judge.

> And when the said road from Middlebury to Woodstock shall be completed, and approved by a committee, consisting of three judicious men to be appointed by the judges of the supreme court, it shall be lawful for said company to erect on said road five turnpike gates, . . . and shall be entitled to receive from each passenger at each of said gates, the fol-

lowing rates of toll; for each coach, phaeton, chariot, or other four wheel pleasure carriage, drawn by two horses, fifty-six cents, and if drawn by more than two horses, ten cents for each additional horse; for each chaise, chair, sulkey, or other two-wheeled pleasure carriage, drawn by one horse, thirty cents; and for each additional horse, nine cents. For each cart or waggon drawn by two oxen or horses, twenty-five cents, and if drawn by more than two oxen or horses, for each additional ox or horse four cents. For each sled or sleigh drawn by two oxen or horses twelve cents and for each additional ox or horse three cents; and if drawn by one horse, eight cents; for every man and horse eight cents; for all horses led or driven, exclusive of those in teams or carriages, if under ten, two and an half cents each, and if over ten, one cent each: For all neat cattle in droves, of the number of ten or under, two cents each, if over ten, one cent for each additional creature; and for all sheep and swine, of the number of twelve, or under, half a cent each, if over twelve, at the rate of three cents per dozen.

All this projected lucrative business was granted with the usual proviso that no person would be obliged to pay any toll on the way to or from church, on the way to and from a grist or sawmill, on militia duty, or "on domestic business of family concerns." A gate keeper knew his clientele well enough to anticipate a minimum of trouble in separating free from paying travelers. Altogether, the anticipated income from a single stagecoach of ten passengers going between Woodstock and Middlebury could be close to thirty dollars. It looked like a paying proposition to anyone who read only the rates of toll and "tollable articles" on the high sign which had to be set up at the entrance.

The Corporation was empowered to erect one gate as soon as a fifth of the road was done and put up new gates as other parts were completed. They could divide the grant into shires, were required to make periodic financial reports to the Secretary of State, and every fifteen years were directed to lay their books before the judges of the Supreme Court, and when the Court could determine that "the toll received shall have paid all the expenses of making, repairing, improving, and taking care of said road, together with an annual interest on the same, at the rate of twelve per centum, then, and in that case, the said supreme court may dissolve said corporation, and thereafter the property of said road shall rest in this state and be at the disposal of the legislature." Six years in which to complete the project were granted.

Gamaliel Painter knew that he was undertaking a formidable project when he accepted the presidency of the Center Turnpike Company. He knew the cut of the land, the streams he had to bypass and the mountains he had to go over. The President did much of the surveying, but the actual building was done by another corporation member with contract specifications to "make all bridges and sluices of good sound green timber or stone, with stone butments for the bridges, . . . the said sluices or water courses to be made at suitable distance from each other to prevent the water from flowing the road, and of sufficient depth and width to carry off the water from the same, and prevent the said road from being wet and spongy by the water standing at the sides of said road. All roots and stumps and stones to be removed out of said road so as to prevent the wheels of carriages from striking them in traveling said road and so that they may not be thrown out by the frost . . . Every part thereof shall be made in such workmanlike and faithful manner as . . . would have been done by any prudent individual owning the whole of said grant."

Painter held the presidency only a short time. His active

participation in the venture was principally during the initial stages of corporation organization and road survey. He recognized the great need for the road, but also foresaw that the income from it would make no one wealthy. Cannily he bought only nine of the three hundred shares of stock offered to the public, while Daniel Chipman eventually secured a controlling interest of over one hundred and fifty shares. Chipman, who owned a sizeable farm along the turnpike in Ripton, and later built a new home near one of the toll gates, was far more interested in the Company than Painter, and he gradually assumed all the administrative responsibilities. The dimensions of the undertaking were far greater than either Painter or Chipman had pictured. Not until 1808 was the last toll gate opened, and any attempt to keep the precipitous road in good repair was discouraged by almost daily washouts. The stagecoach from Hanover, New Hampshire, was routed over it, but the passengers preferred to walk up the mountain behind the coach rather than risk their lives aboard it. In less than a decade after the completion of the road, the Center Turnpike Company began to exhibit signs of bankruptcy, and, without too much reluctance, it started relinquishing its holdings, gate by gate, to the Legislature.

But Painter, meantime, had become involved in a more lucrative venture, the key stretch of road between Middlebury and Vergennes, labeled by Assembly act "The Waltham Turnpike." Anyone passing north or south through the central part of Champlain Valley would virtually have to patronize his road. Gamaliel Painter was again the chairman and spokesman for his corporation of six partners. The terms of the charter were similar to those for the Center Turnpike, but only one gate was authorized for the fifteen miles, and the rate per passenger was somewhat lower: "For every four wheeled pleasure carriage (other than waggons with spring seats) drawn by two beasts, forty cents, for every additional beast five cents; for every two wheeled pleasure carriage, drawn by one beast, twenty cents, and for each additional beast, five cents; for each waggon or cart, the felloes whereof shall be eight inches or more in breadth, drawn by two beasts, six cents . . . ," down to sleds and sleighs drawn by two beasts for six and a quarter cents, and sheep or swine at three cents a dozen. The new system of basing toll on the width of the wheel rims or felloes had just come into vogue, and, lest there be any restraint of heavy trade, waggons with felloes of six inches were to be permitted to pass toll free for four years; those with felloes of eight inches or more were to pass free for eight years. These monstrous wheels, frequently ten and twelve feet high, supporting loads of ten tons, were ideal road conditioners. The military and the churchgoers could not be assessed; nor in fact could any state resident living within a radius of eight miles, since they had already done time in taxes for its start.

The owners were protected against the short tempers of the long-suffering public with the regulation that "if any person or persons shall cut, break down, or otherwise destroy, any of said turnpike gates, or signs . . . or attempt to pass by force any of said gates, without first having paid the legal toll at such gate, such person . . . shall pay all damages . . . and pay a fine not exceeding fifty dollars." The owners were protected, too, against those who made a practice of evading the gate keeper and following the shunpike: "If any person with his carriage, cattle or horse, shall turn out of said road, to pass any of the turnpike gates, and again enter the said road . . . such person shall forfeit and pay three times as much as his legal toll would have been."

Despite the large number of people who managed free passage, the owners of the Waltham Turnpike made money. It was mostly from tourist trade, commercial men and immigrants, but the income was one of the sources of the modest fortune which Painter was accumulating. As consultant for turnpikes, as part owner of the Turnpike to Hubbardton, and investor in others, he had still further revenue. By 1815 some fifty turnpikes crisscrossed the State. There were long ones with five gates, like the Windham Turnpike between Bennington and Brattleborough, which cost a passenger $2.75 traveling in a four-wheeled carriage drawn by two horses; like the Green Mountain Turnpike between Clarendon and Bellows Falls which cost $2.64; and the Center with a charge of $2.80. But most of the turnpikes were with single or dual gates, and the distance traveled between the gates had little relation to the assessment. The two-gate Manchester Company received $1.50 for each passenger in a pleasure carriage drawn by a span of horses between Manchester and Chester, whereas the four-gate Connecticut River Company between Bellows Falls and Thetford charged $1.36, and the single-gate Hubbardton Company for nearly as long a trip between Sudbury and Castleton received fifty-six cents. In whatever direction one traveled he ran into the web of turnpikes ready to relieve a passenger of forty-four cents, or of ninety-four, thirty, thirty-one, fifty-six and a quarter cents, a dollar, to the enrichment of the Mad River Company between Hancock and the Winooski River, the Mount Taber between Danby and Manchester, the Sandbar between Colchester and the Lake, the Winooski between Burlington and Montpelier, or the Boston and Montreal from the Connecticut River to the Canadian Line.

Town treasurers had seen that they could make ends meet more easily by having roads privately financed and Surveyors of Highways had gladly accepted relief from their thankless duties as collectors of taxes in the form of labor, but the citizenry began to question the wisdom of their enthusiasm for so readily giving up their rights to roads. Travel was becoming an expensive luxury, and Painter and other capitalists who controlled that luxury were an abomination. Every eight or ten miles of travel was broken by a halt at a gate to forfeit cash for tolls that would better have been paid in cash for taxes. Better roads had been built, and many were a service to local residents who were not required to subsidize them, but travel expense for outsiders was prohibitive. A circuitous route of less than two hundred miles from Brattleboro to Burlington, via a series of six turnpikes, could cost a family of five close to fifty dollars in tolls alone.

In his eagerness to promote good thoroughfares and reap the profits, Painter broke all precedent in Vermont for road covetousness by sponsoring one petition to the Assembly for a turnpike to end all turnpikes, stretching the entire distance from Pownal in the southwest corner of the State to Highgate in the northwest corner. It would have cut through all the eastern counties, and run from the Massachusetts line to Canada, over three hundred miles. It would have created a preposterous monopoly and made Painter one of the magnates of his day. But the Legislature recognized an element of greediness in the scheme, and charitably gave him an opportunity to withdraw the petition before the representatives had a chance to voice their disapproval. His dream of a trunk line turnpike vanished. Other dreams of fortunes in turnpikes vanished too, and in the following years the public reversed itself to favor taxation in place of tolls, but by that time, Painter had put away his earnings.

CIVIL ENGINEER

As an artificer, Captain Painter had been exposed to every phase of engineering, from transportation and sanitary engineering to architecture and mechanics. His engineering education was in the laboratory of experience. He won great fame for his company and his regiment. At Middlebury he translated his talents principally into industrial and civil works, though the tasks to be accomplished were far more limited in scope than those that confronted him in service. He was a builder of bridges and public structures; he harnessed water power; he designed and constructed mills; and he had a hand in surveying and constructing most of the highways of the county. His greatest contribution was in road building. All of the engineering was in the interest of public welfare. On some of his projects he made money, and appeared to be taking advantage of a public need, but in the end practically every dollar of it went back to the public from which it was taken.

12 PHILANTHROPIST

During the second decade of the 1800's, Middlebury developed into the largest and most substantial community west of the Green Mountains. Woodstock, Hartland, Windsor, and Springfield, grouped together east of the mountains near the Connecticut River, were the only towns in the State which closely rivaled it. The 1820 census gave Middlebury a population of 2535 and the four Connecticut River towns an average of 2700, but industrially Middlebury was ahead. Communities like Burlington and Bennington, Rutland and Montpelier, Brattleboro and Bellows Falls were all behind commercially, industrially, socially, numerically. No one disputed any longer the wisdom of Painter's choice for the town site. His speculation in land, his convictions on the worth of manufacturing, his influence in high places and low, his devotion to causes cultural and spiritual had borne fruit many fold.

At the beginning of the decade, Timothy Dwight paid another visit to Middlebury and reported: "I found Middlebury changed into a beautiful town, consisting of about one hundred and fifty houses. The inhabitants have finished a large and handsome church. The private buildings are generally neat, and in several instances, handsome. The town contains a bookstore, a printing office, twelve or fifteen stores belonging to merchants and druggists, and a great number of mechanics shops . . . Religion has prevailed in this town more than in any other in the State, and controls very obviously the manners, and the character of the inhabitants, in a degree uncommon and delightful. Its influence is very happily seen in the College; where the best order prevails, under a discipline, exact, indeed, but mild and parental. Upon the whole, Middlebury is one of the most prosperous, and most virtuous towns in New England."

Toward the *end* of the decade, Professor Hall, instructor of Natural Philosophy at the College, strode through the village, notebook in hand, and made an unofficial tally of what he saw: 196 dwelling houses, six of brick, the rest of wood; three meetinghouses; two college buildings, one of wood the other of stone; thirty-three manufactories constructed of wood, four of stone; thirteen stores, six of wood and seven of brick, a courthouse; an academy of wood; a stone jail; a brick schoolhouse: total number of buildings, 604.

"The village now contains," he recapitulated, "one printing office, at which is printed a respectable weekly paper, seven English and India goods stores, one apothecary store, one bookstore, three taverns, one woolen factory, two grist and two saw mills, one stone mill, one trip hammer shop, two cotton factories, thirteen law offices and four physicians.

"In 1820, the number of mechanics' shops in the village was as follows, viz: three hatters' shops, six shoemakers', two tailors', four milliners', three saddlers', two goldsmiths', one clothier's, seven blacksmiths', one gunsmith's, one glazier's, four wheelwrights', one painter's, two coopers', two tinmen's, two potteries, two potashes, three tanneries, two cabinet makers', two bakehouses, nine joiners', and four masons . . .

"The marble . . . machinery is propelled by water and puts in motion sixty-five saws . . . The marble is quarried within a stone's throw of the manufactory and is of various colours. Since the company was incorporated the annual amount of the manufactures of this article has been from $6000 to $8000 . . . One of the cotton factories in this village contained 840 spindles and fifteen power looms, or looms moved by water, and the other, 600 spindles and fifteen power looms . . . There is probably no other village in the state, which equals this in the extent of its manufactories, and none which surpasses it in liberality and public spirit."

This was the town which Painter had created, and in his mature years he could stroll across the front yard of his spacious house and survey it all in well-earned satisfaction. He was the squire. But his energy and his demand for action, even in his advanced years, permitted no dotage. Like other men who have a reluctance to make any display of emotion, he was utterly dependent on intimate human warmth. The death of Vicca had left an intolerable void of loneliness. He could accept the affection and respect of his colleagues and associates, and he had the devotion of his daughter, Abby Victoria, but he needed the more intimate counsel and closeness of a wife. The great house was a vacuum without her. And once more he introduced to Middlebury a stalwart, unaffected woman from southern New England. She was an elderly widow, Mrs. Ursula Bull, whose former husband had been a distinguished Connecticut senator. The great household brightened. The gaiety of former days returned. Painter discovered a new humor. The genuineness of the old couple endeared them to the community. They made a place in their home for the young as well as the elderly. There was no show or pomp. Together they crossed the village green to attend church, seeking no homage for their position in the community and recognizing none. Together they went to College disputations at the Courthouse, where a casual word was passed to a student whom the trustee had helped with a term bill, or another who had boarded with them one winter. Occasionally he sat in on a court session and quietly admired the jurisprudence of younger men which he modestly knew he never matched in his youth. The elder still belonged to youth, and his daughter Abby Victoria brought the vitality of youth close to them.

Abby, now about twenty, was the treasure of his life. She symbolized for him a kind of triumph over the years of struggle he had known and the suffering that went with them. She was the one link with the missing members of the family. In her he saw Sama and Joseph and Victoria, and even Abigail. The two had been inseparable during the grief-stricken weeks and months after Victoria's death, and even after Ursula came, Painter's attachment for his daughter was unchanged. Daughters of other families who could afford it had been sent away to school, but Painter was so devoted to Abby that he could not permit her out of his sight. She had received her first schooling at Emma Willard's Seminary, never realizing that it was the best in New England; and later Eliza Page had been invited to bring her school into Gamaliel Painter's own home. Abby had studied most of the subjects that were offered to the underclassmen at the College: ancient and modern geography, grammar, arithmetic, writing, history, rhetoric, natural and moral philosophy, astronomy, chemistry and logic. On the side she had devoted classroom time to what every cultivated girl in her teens was expected to know: drawing, painting, embroidery, dancing, music and French. She was a charming girl, the belle of the town, though somewhat distant, and given to religion. Her hobby was history, and her spare time was spent in reading omnivorously every available book on ancient and medieval civilization. "Few persons of her years," commented one appraiser of her merit, "have gained so thorough, and extensive an insight into the history of the world . . . She did not read, like most others, for amusement only, but for the sake of treasuring up in her memory that kind of knowledge which would render her more interesting and respectable in the world."

Her whole life, however, was changed during the summer of 1815, following one of the religious revivals which burst upon the town periodically. Abby, classing herself with town infidels, suddenly realized "her perishing condition, . . . felt that she was a sinner, that she had offended a holy and just God, that she had no merit in herself; that her heart was the seat of native and acquired corruption." She had the self-righteousness as well as the stubborn determination of her father, convinced herself that the Episcopal church had more to offer than the Congregational, and true to her convictions, left her father's church to join the Episcopalians. For a time it was the subject of scandalous village talk, but when it was discovered that Gamaliel warmly honored her right to choose her own denomination and that the talk served no purpose, the gossip subsided. Abby helped to found the Middlebury Female Bible Society, became its president, and expended her energies on good works.

Not to be outdone by his daughter, Painter took a new lease on religion, and in the same year, at the age of 73, formed "The Addison County Society for the Suppression of Vice and the Promotion of Good Morals." The new organization, of which he was president, was based on the premises that "iniquity is grossly prevalent; the Law of God is trampled under foot. Our own penal statutes have become less than a dead letter. The Sabbath is widely and wantonly profaned. Intemperate use of ardent spirits is making fearful ravages. Gaming is widely practised. The language of profaneness is heard in our streets, in our public houses and in almost every promiscuous assemblage." The purpose of the organization was to revolutionize morals "by example and reprimand."

But Painter did not spend all his time suppressing vice, and reprimanding the evildoers. He was disposing of the last of his land in the Winooski valley—without the aid of an agent. He was involved in more village organizations than there were hours in a day and days in a week. He was a corporation member of the Vermont Agricultural Society, a charter member of the Fire Society, Master Mason at the Union Lodge, Vice President of the Middlebury Charitable Society. On occasion he still had to break out the remnants of his Captain's uniform to participate in celebrations and parades. He was in demand as a member of every type of civic committee. There were constant board or committee meetings for the Congregational church, meetings of the College trustees, meetings of the Grammar School board. There was never a day unbroken by visitors calling on him for advice, consultation and judgment. His measured imprint had been left in every corner of the county; newcomers discovered it and came to him to conjure up a recollection, settle an argument, confirm a suspicion. The birch trees and the white hazel staddles with which he had butted and bounded his surveys had rotted away and lines needed to be reëstablished; the corner heap of stones had been lost in the underbrush; the pine stumps had disintegrated; and the walnut trees had sprouted younger walnut trees which were confused with the original. Painter was given few minutes of peace, and he reveled in the lack of peace. Inaction he could not endure.

He had developed an enthusiasm for horse breeding, knowing that a finer breed of horse would be a great boon to the agriculture of Vermont. He had started with his prize animal, *Active*, and advertised in the local press: "The Noted Horse ACTIVE stands at Gamaliel Painter's stable to be let to mares at ten dollars the season, and seven dollars the single leap—Wheat, Corn, Oats will be received for pay, if delivered by the first of January next." Other farmers did not fully appreciate the value of improving horses and were reluctant to patronize the high prices for service, but Painter was convinced and purchased the famous full-blooded Arabian "Young Dey of Algiers." Even the Albany press considered Young Dey "the greatest acquisition to our breed of horses which the country has ever gained since the importation of Ranger."

No matter how occupied he was, however, with personal hobbies, vice prevention, turnpikes and the Masons, he always had time for his first avocation, the College. Middlebury College needed him sorely during its second decade of existence. The institution had been so successful that it was crowding itself out of the Academy building. It needed additional classrooms, new laboratories, new student quarters, a larger library. To make matters more critical, the trustees had found it necessary to increase the President's salary to $1100, and professors were expecting compensation equal to what the President previously received. Then the President's salary had to be increased by another $200 "in consideration of the depreciation of the circulating currency and the extra expenses of living," and to offset bids to the presidency of Hamilton and Yale he had to be granted a loan of $3,000 as an "indispensably necessary provision for his family." New professorships were being introduced, scholarships had to be provided, upkeep of buildings was proving expensive. The tuition of $14.00 could scarcely begin to cover expenses. The College needed money, and Painter was drafted to get it.

A long session with the Legislature brought flattering commentary regarding the "flourishing state of that seminary . . . wholly built up and supported by individual beneficence . . . having arrived at a state of usefulness and importance," but it brought no money: "Your committee . . . beg leave to report, that they have . . . duly weighed the importance of the subject of giving, at this time, some legislative aid to Middlebury College and that it is with extreme regret your committee cannot devise any mode . . . by which said College can, at this time, receive any pecuniary aid."

One well-meaning legislator, impressed with the worthiness of Painter's appeals, earnestly proposed that a lottery might furnish a way out for the College: "Resolved that it is expedient to provide for raising by lottery the sum of————

dollars, for the purpose of enabling the President and Fellows of Middlebury College, without burdensome advances from individuals, to maintain said institution upon a footing, honorable to the State, and useful to the young and growing population of our country."

The resolution was read, adopted, referred to a committee, tabled, amended, retabled. There were those who considered operating a lottery inconsistent with the moral principles of a college. Again and again, Painter and others went to the Legislature for help, and they were a long time in discovering that help was not to come from that source. In one attempt to get the allegiance and moral support of the Legislature, the trustees voted to alter the charter to admit the Governor, the Lt. Governor, the Speaker and the Secretary of State as ex-officio members of the board, and when they learned that the University of Vermont was discussing the possibility of a union with Middlebury as something "desirable for the interest of learning in this state," they hastily, but guardedly, appointed three representatives to confer "on the interesting subject and report the opinion of the practicability of such a measure."

In the end the trustees conceded that they would have to work out their own financial salvation, and the venerable Painter was the proper messenger. As early as October, 1810, the Corporation voted succinctly "that a College edifice be erected on the ground lately conveyed to the President and Fellows of Middlebury College by Col. Seth Storrs, and that the subscriptions for building the college be collected by the Treasurer and applied to that purpose." On second thought, they added "that Gamaliel Painter be agent for the Corporation to erect the new college building. . . ."

Painter accepted the agency, but learned shortly that a construction agent had small chance of success without construction funds. The engineer took on the additional assignment of fund raising. Appeals were broadcast in the town and in the environs of the town. Promises started to trickle in, and just when reasonable hope of success appeared, there arose an argument with which Painter once had long experience: What was the most desirable location for the new school? the east side of the creek, or the west side? Promises were made that land east of the creek would be provided equal in area to what Storrs had given on the west. That gave both sides an equal handicap, and the crafty fund raiser proceeded to take advantage of it, playing off one side against the other. Subscription forms were supplied for the eastsiders and separate subscription forms were supplied for the westsiders. Those who promised the largest amount would win a college. As referee, Painter had his problems, for subscriptions came in every kind of currency: nails, teamwork, merchandise, pew number 18 in the Congregational Church, lumber, marble, plaster, labor, joiner's work, stone, carpenters' work, timber, glass, pew number 84, store goods, brick, sawn stone, a thousand feet of pine boards, boots and shoes, real estate, roofing, firewood. There were substantial subscriptions in money, too: one promise of a thousand dollars, two $500's, several hundreds, and a long list of modest subscriptions, ranging from five dollars up. But the concentrated wealth seemed to favor Storrs' old farm site: the westsiders won. And Painter, true to character, then talked conciliation to the opponents and persuaded most of them to apply their promises to the venture on the hillside north of the Academy building.

With the accumulation of all the lumber, stone, nails, glass and labor at his disposal, actual erection of the new college

228

was a minor operation for the old artificer. West College with its thirty-six fireplaces and elegant rooms for students, built of the same kind of limestone used for the mills, the jail, and other institutional buildings in town, became the showplace of the town, though years elapsed before the building was given the name of Painter Hall, to honor the man who was responsible for its construction.

Even before the new college was completed, Painter was at work on an endowment drive to ease the College out of other indebtedness. His name was at the top of the list with a thousand dollar pledge for a campaign of $20,000. In fact, few subscription lists were complete without his name leading all the rest: an initial $500 for the College building, $30 for a bonus to the President, $10 for a professorship of Mathematics and Philosophy; "I engage to guarantee one tenth part of the said four hundred dollars, to Mr. Hall, for ten years, agreeable to the within writing, Gaml. Painter."

As Vice President of the Charitable Society, he was constantly giving funds and soliciting funds for indigent students who wished to enter the ministry: "The Middlebury College Charitable Society, established for the purpose of liberally educating young gentlemen for the Gospel ministry, think proper to call the attention of the publick to the objects they have in view, and respectfully solicit their countenance and cooperation . . . Nearly one hundred towns in this state, and probably about the same proportion in the adjoining states, are destitute of preachers of any description . . . No method presents itself to the society so likely to be effective to this end, as that of giving encouragement to young gentlemen of apparent piety and belonging to some Christian church, in obtaining a collegiate education."

His labor did not go unappreciated, even by students. With sharp wit and insight, one undergraduate put into doggerel his summary of Middlebury's problem and blessings:

> Within these walls I flew with quickened pace,
> To read her Charter and inspect the place.
> But sad to tell, I read her Charter o'er
> Again I read it—and again once more—
> I saw, alas, no Legislative hand
> Enroll the Fiat—yet for ages stand.
> No bounteous Fund her annual tribute bring,
> To enrich the walls with every needed thing.
> I saw no Patron's wealth for years to come,
> Ensure to fill her Philosophic room;
> . . .
> But I still saw what gave my soul to taste
> Of purest joy a rich enchanting feast,
> A Patriot band, my favorite sons I call,
> In zeal abundant, yet in number small,
> Combine with willing heart and lib'ral hand
> To raise yon College dome to bless the land.
> High on the list, I saw a fav'rite name,
> Dear to his country, and to well-earned fame;
> . . .
> A Painter rich in merited esteem,
> The wise contriver of each deep-laid scheme,
> Whose every step sound policy attends,
> And points the surest means to purpos'd ends.

From academic affairs Painter still kept his distance. His scholarship did not improve with his exposure to scholars, and his spelling continued to be phonetic; medicine was *medison*, perfect was *parfact*, struggle became *strugel*, audience *audiance*, journey *jurney* and the Courthouse he had helped build was a *Cort House*. His knowledge of surveying, mechanics and

230

geology brought the field of mathematics and natural philosophy nearest to his comprehension, but although the trustees granted each other honorary degrees, there were evident reservations about awarding Painter a doctorate in science. The chores given him by the corporation were non-academic and dealt almost exclusively with material problems. When a Medical Department was established, it was Gamaliel Painter who was elected "a committee of one to prepare a lecture room and to assist Dr. Smith in procuring a house for his family." Painter was on the Committee "to communicate with General Arad Hunt, and receive a conveyance from him to the Corporation of any property he may be disposed to bestow upon the College." Painter was always among those requested to intercede with the Legislature. It was he who was employed to investigate facilities for establishing a dining commons, or reconstructing a room "for the receipt of minerals." His counsel was so valuable that in the late years of his life, when it was difficult for him to attend corporation meetings in the College Library, the trustees met at his home. The Painter residence became the recognized meeting place for the Board. Old age was kind to him, but a weight on his shoulders was pronounced, and his short even stride became unsteady. The settle in his front room was his post, and when he could no longer go to others, they came to him. His home was the nucleus of the village.

In the summer of 1818, his daughter Abby Victoria developed a suspicious and persistent cough. Painter consulted the College professors and his close medical friends. Even the kindest of them shook their heads and mentioned consumption. They prescribed activity and change of scenery when she should have remained quiet, travel when she should have been confined to her room. Their injudicious advice was followed.

231

She made a long journey to Connecticut and was convinced that she benefited from it; but from another trip to Granville she returned in a state of collapse. During the late summer and autumn she lay in her room, completely resigned to the inevitable, expounding the benefits of the spiritual life to anyone who would listen, praying incessantly and begging others to pray for her. She was convinced that the illness was a divine visitation. "Mama, I do not now desire you to pray that I will get well," she told Mrs. Painter, "but that I may honor God while I live, and particularly in my last hour." In morbid agony she explained, "I do not allow myself to think of my body's moulding in the grave, for then death would be a gloomy subject. 'Tis my immortal part, that I wish to think upon . . . Evil speaking has been my besetting sin, always . . . Religion has been all my consolation in my sickness . . . My Saviour —my all—my Saviour, strengthen me to pass through the dark valley of the shadow of death . . . The joys of heaven brighten and brighten the nearer I approach them. I see my Saviour ready to receive me . . ." Her prayer and preachment drifted off into incoherence, and late in the afternoon of the ninth of December, 1818, she passed away.

The whole town joined with her father in mourning, and one anonymous poetaster contributed the lines:

> We sought to know the mournful tale,
> To mark the exit of the spirit fled;
> We hear the voice of sorrow's wail
> We hear the sob—Victoria's dead.
> . . .
> Farewell Victoria—nature's child—
> Thou child of hope redeem'd by love:
> On thee has mercy ever smiled,
> And smiles in brighter joys above.

Painter was beside himself with grief. Abby Victoria had been the supreme joy and satisfaction of his old age. When he craved the verve and excitement of youth about him, she had supplied it. Her understanding and rich imagination had meant everything to him. Death had tagged some close member of the family every few years all his life; his brothers, his parents, his first wife, his two sons, his second wife, and now his daughter. The last was too much to bear. The powerful shoulders stooped under the weight of grief. Courage was gone from him. The death of Abby Victoria was his death. In failing health and in sad reflection, he went through the motions of life during the winter and early spring of 1819.

On May 12th he summoned Dr. Boss and two other neighbors to witness the will he had inscribed:

May 12, 1819.
In the name of GOD—Amen.
I, Gamaliel Painter of the Town of Middlebury in the County of Addison and State of Vermont, being weak in body, but of sound and perfect mind and memory, do make and publish this my last will and testament in manner and form following: That is to say,—Imprimis—

I give to my beloved wife Ursula Painter the sum of two hundred dollars, to be paid her annually, during her natural life, by my executors hereinafter named; also the use of one third of my dwelling house and garden during the same term. I likewise give her for her use and disposal, one third of my household furniture; and also my chaise and black horse.

Item—I give to my sister Sarah Williams of New Haven in the State of Connecticut, one hundred dollars to be paid her annually during her life by the executors of this my last will and testament.

Lastly, as to all the rest, residue and remainder of my estate either real or personal, of what kind or nature soever (after the payment of my just debts) I give the same to President & Fellows of Middlebury College and their successors forever . . .

The College's share of the estate would total some $13,000—a saving fortune for the destitute institution, and he modestly recommended that it "be appropriated to the building of a new College in due time."

The end came quickly and kindly less than two weeks later. There was no need to publish a local obituary. Everyone in Middlebury knew the story of Painter. In crisp understatement, the National Standard made the announcement:

> DIED—In this town, on the 21st inst. the Hon. Gamaliel Painter, aged 76—leaving an aged widow and sister, and many friends to lament his loss.
>
> Judge Painter was a captain in the revolutionary war; was the first person who moved a family into Middlebury; has for many years been considered the father of the town, and a patron of its constitution. He was one of the Fellows of Middlebury College; often contributed liberally to aid its funds, and by his last will and testament, after making provision by a annuity for his widow and sister, bequeathed to the College the whole of the valuable estate which he had been acquiring for many years. . . . His remains were interred with Masonic honors.

The College Trustees appropriated the larger portion of his bequest, $10,000, "for the purpose of supporting forever the Professorship of Mathematics and Natural Philosophy which in honor of this greatly respected patron of science, shall hereafter be denominated 'The Painter Professorship of Mathematics and Natural Philosophy.'" At his grave the College also erected a monument with the citation: "He was a patriot of

234

the Revolution, faithful in civil office, and amicable in private life; distinguished for decision, enterprise and public spirit." Even these words engraved in stone failed remarkably to estimate his wealth of character and the devotion of a life to the founding of a town and a college.

GAMALIEL PAINTER'S CANE

Charles B. Wright
E. Pruda Wiley '12

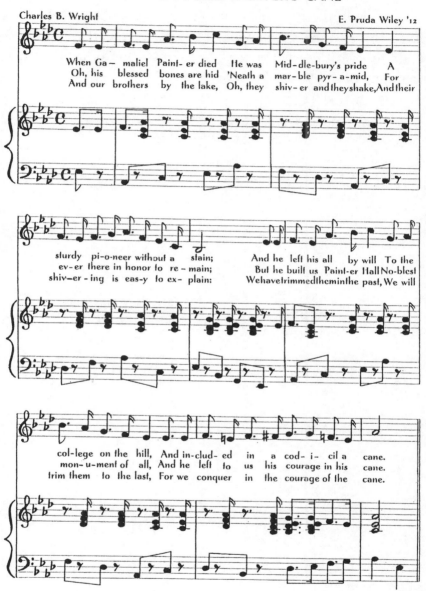

When Ga—maliel Paint-er died He was Mid—dle-bury's pride A
Oh, his blessed bones are hid 'Neath a mar—ble pyr—a-mid, For
And our brothers by the lake, Oh, they shiv—er and they shake, And their

sturdy pi-o-neer without a stain; And he left his all by will To the
ev—er there in honor to re—main; But he built us Paint-er Hall No-blest
shiv—er-ing is eas-y to ex—plain: We have trimmed them in the past, We will

col-lege on the hill, And in-clud-ed in a cod-i-cil a cane.
mon—u-ment of all, And he left to us his courage in his cane.
trim them to the last, For we conquer in the courage of the cane.

CHORUS

Oh, it's rap - rap - rap, And it's tap - tap - tap, If you list - en you can hear it sound-ing plain; For a help - er true and tried, As the gen - er - a - tions glide, There is noth - ing like Ga - ma - liel Paint-er's cane.

REFERENCE SOURCES

CHAPTER ONE

pp. 5-7, Middlebury Charter. Ms. Town Clerk's Office, Middlebury; pp. 7 ff., Middlebury town meetings. Swift, Samuel, *History of Middlebury*, Middlebury, 1859, pp. 147-152; pp. 8, 9, Winthrop on Painter. Hosmer, J. K. (Editor) *Winthrop's Journal—History of New England 1630–1749*, Vol. II, p. 177; p. 9, Shubael's record. Jacobus, D. L. "The Painter Family," *New England Historical and Genealogical Register*, July 1914, p. 273; p. 15, "We must master . . ." Miller, J. C. *Origins of the American Revolution*, p. 356; p. 16, Deed. *Land Records 1763–73*. Ms. Town Clerk's Office, Salisbury, Conn., Vol. IV, p. 593; Quitclaim. Ibid., p. 612; p. 20, "buts and bounds." Swift, Samuel, op. cit., p. 159.

CHAPTER TWO

p. 26, Letter from Allen to N. Y. Governor. Slade, William. *Vermont State Papers*, p. 32; p. 29, "Grants or confirmations . . ." Ibid., p. 36; "many acts of outrage . . ." Ibid., pp. 42, 43; "if any person . . ." Ibid., p. 45; p. 31, Artillery at Ticonderoga. Force, Peter. *American Archives*, Fourth Series, Vol. II, col. 450; Arnold's orders. Ibid., col. 485; p. 35, Arnold's letter. Ibid., col. 557; p. 36, Allen's letter to Mass. Ibid., col. 507; Allen's letter to N. Y. Ibid., col. 606; p. 37, "wild, impractical scheme." Ltr. Arnold to Mass. Com. of Safety, May 19, 1775. Ibid., col. 645; p. 40, Washington's reprimand to Allen. Fitzpatrick, John C. (Editor) *Writings of George Washington*, Vol. IV, p. 46; Elisha's complaint. Force, Peter. op. cit., Vol. IV, Col. 1049; p. 41, Letter to Continental Congress. Slade, William. op. cit., p. 64; p. 42, Baldwin on Bunker Hill, Baldwin, Charles C. *The Baldwin Genealogy from 1500 to 1880*, p. 626; Baldwin on Canadian expedition. Baldwin, Thomas W. (Editor). *Revolutionary Journal of Colonel Jeduthan Baldwin 1775–1778*, pp. 45-52; pp. 42 ff. Baldwin's diary. Ibid., pp. 62, 63; p. 44, Commissions for Warner's regiment. *Journals of Continental Congress*, Vol. V., p. 518; p. 45, Warner's letter to Continental Congress. Force, Peter. op. cit., Fifth series, Vol. II, col. 273; Elisha's orders to Philadelphia. *Journals of Continental Congress*, Vol. V, p. 754; p. 47, Dorset resolution. Slade, William. op. cit., p. 67; Vermont declaration of independence. Ibid., pp. 69-70; p. 48, Painter as spy. Swift, Samuel. op. cit., pp. 186, 187; pp. 49, 50, Evacuation of Ticonderoga. Baldwin, T. W. op. cit., p. 109; p. 50, First Constitution. Slade, William. op. cit., p. 241.

CHAPTER THREE

p. 54, Elisha Painter's evaluation of his services. Force, Peter. *American Archives*, Vol. III, cols. 1136-7; Clean bill of health. Ibid.; Congressional resolution on Elisha. *Journals of Continental Congress*, Vol. 7, p. 48; p. 55, Riders to Congressional resolution. Ibid., p. 298; p. 56, Pay for Artificers. *Writings of Washington*, Vol. III, p. 506; Congressional approval of employment of Artificers. *Journals of Continental Congress*, Vol. III, p. 400; p. 57, Knox on "the best men." *Papers of George Washington*, Ms. Library of Congress, Vol. 37, p. 108; Composition of company of Artificers. *Writings of Washington*. Vol. VII, p. 20; p. 59, Enticement for recruits. "Instructions to the Officer Appointed to Recruit." Flier. Fishkill, N. Y., Nov. 21, 1776. Ms. V. A. National Archives, Washington, D C.; Instructions for Recruiting Officer. Ibid.; p. 60, Army regulations. *Journals of Continental Congress*, Articles of War, Vol. II, pp. 111-122; p. 61, Washington's order of June 18, 1778. Myers, W. S. *Stryker's Battle of Monmouth*, p. 63; pp. 61, 62, Oath of allegiance. *Journals of Continental Congress*, Vol. IV, p. 66; p. 62, British procession of retreat. Myers, W. S. op. cit., p. 90; Lafayette's comment. Ibid., p. 185; p. 63, Orders of Commander-in-Chief on Artificers and pioneers. Ibid., pp. 70-71; "Clearly superior to any fighting men . . ." Ibid., p. 238; p. 64, Wiccopee Pass. *American Guide Series, Dutchess County*. Compiled by FWPA 1937, p. 80; "a miserable shelter . . ." Auburey, Thomas. *Travels Through The Interior Parts of America*, Vol. II, p. 153; pp. 65, 66, "the number of applications . . ." *Writings of Washington*, Vol. XII, p. 65; p. 66, "the draughts for the Army . . ." Ibid.; Washington's order to Quartermaster General. Ibid., p. 422; Washington's order to West Point. Ibid., Vol. XVI, p. 255; p. 67, Elisha Painter's Court-Martial verdict. Ibid., Vol. XIII, p. 73; Elisha's letter to Washington. *Papers of George Washington*. 1778, Vol. 88, Ms. Library of Congress; Washington's order for new trial. *Writings of Washington*, Vol. 13, p. 189; p. 68, Elisha's letter to Arnold. *Papers of George Washington*, Vol. 146, 1780, Aug. 12-18. Ms. Library of Congress; Elisha Painter's will. Ms. Connecticut State Library, Hartford; Elisha Painter's possessions. "Inventory of Elisha Painter's Estate." Ms. Connecticut State Library; Hannah's appeal. *Connecticut Archives, Revolutionary War*, Vol. XXV, p. 2; p. 69, Request of Board of War to Congress. *Papers of the Continental Congress*, Reports of the Board of War, Vol. III, pp. 365-371. Ms. Dept. of State Library, Washington; p. 70, Painter's letter to Arnold. *Papers of George Washington*, Vol. 150, p. 77. Ms. Library of Congress; p. 71, Bett's endorsement. Ibid., p. 73; Arnold's reply. *Peter Force Transcripts* No. 3436. Ms. Library of Congress; p. 72, Washington's order to Hay. *Writings of Washington*, Vol. XXI, p. 2; "not a drop of Rum . . ." Ibid., Vol. XXII, p. 182; pp. 72 ff, Letter Painter to Pickering: War Department (transferred from State Dept.). National Archives. Document 25392. Ms.;

REFERENCE SOURCES

p. 75, Col. Baldwin's orders. War Department (transferred from State Dept.) 123. War of the Revolution Letters of Col. Pickering 1780–1781. Ms.; "Among the many things . . ." *Writings of Washington*, Vol. XXI, p. 41; Washington's complaint to Pickering. *Writings of Washington*, Vol. XXI, p. 41; p. 76, Hides for mending. Ltr. Baldwin to Pickering, Dec. 30, 1780. War Department (transferred from State Dept.) 123. War of the Revolution Letters of Col. Pickering 1780–1781. Ms.; Painter's inquiry to Congress. *Journals of Continental Congress*, Vol. XIX, pp. 324-330; "in a very destitute situation . . ." Ibid., p. 537; p. 77, Washington's order of April 20, 1782. *Writings of Washington*, Vol. XXIV, p. 137.

CHAPTER FOUR

p. 85, "He would never be contented . . ." Swift, Samuel, op. cit., p. 198; Foot's characterization. Perkins, Nathan. *Narrative of a Tour through Vermont*, 1789, p. 16; pp. 86, 87, Description of settlers. Ibid., pp. 18, 19; p. 87, Arcadian life. Merrill, Thomas. *Semicentennial Sermon* 1840; pp. 88 ff., Pioneer household industry. *Cabinet of Useful Arts and Manufactures*. Published by Caleb Bartlett. New York, 1827; pp. 93, 94, The Mill lot. Swift, Samuel. op. cit., p. 162.

CHAPTER FIVE

p. 98, "A day, an hour . . ." Addison, Joseph. *Cato*, Act II; pp. 99 ff. Duties of sheriff. *Vermont State Papers*. Compiled by William Slade 1823, pp. 348-51; pp. 103 ff., Court records. *Records of the County of Addison*. Ms. County Clerk's Office, Middlebury, Book I, pp. 83-87; p. 106, "Bill for levying tax." *Journals of the General Assembly of the State of Vermont*, 1787, p. 38; p. 108, Special bill on Painter. *Statutes of the State of Vermont*, 1787, p. 207; pp. 110, 111, Bartholomew poem. Swift, Samuel. op. cit., p. 241.

CHAPTER SIX

p. 114, Authority of County Court. *Laws of the State of Vermont*, 1788, p. 72; p. 115, Town meeting 1788. Swift, Samuel. op. cit., p. 403; p. 116, Foot's fine. *Book of Records*, Jan. 25, 1790. Ms. Town Clerk's Office, Middlebury; Division of Addison County. *State Papers of Vermont*. Vol. 3 (IV), p. 12; also *Statutes of the State of Vermont* 1787, p. 42; p. 117, "This is the place . . ." Swift, Samuel. op. cit., p. 284; pp. 118 ff. Court appointments. *Records of the County of Addison*, Vol. 1787. Ms. Addison County Clerk's Office; pp. 119, 120, Cases. *Records of the County of Addison*, Ms. Vol. 1; pp. 121, 122, Charges. "Court Records Prior to 1798" Ms. County Clerk's Office; p. 123, Location of Courthouse. *State Papers of Vermont* Vol. 4, p. 71; p. 124, Description of Famine. Perkins, Nathan. op. cit., pp. 21, 22; p. 125, "Such as had strength . . ." Swift, Samuel. op. cit., p. 229; "and after the cows . . ." Ibid., p. 230; p. 126, Mrs. Painter's letter. Ms. Sheldon Museum; p. 127, Subscriptions for College. *State Papers of Vermont*, Vol. 3 (IV), p. 138; p. 128, Committee on church location. Swift, Samuel, op. cit., p. 306; "hardy Green Mountain Boys . . ." Dean, Leon W. *Admission of Vermont into the Union*, p. 41; p. 129, Settlement with New York. State Papers of Vermont Vol. 3 (IV), p. 256; also *Journals of the Assembly* 1790, p. 39; "authorizing the people . . ." Ibid., p. 45.

CHAPTER SEVEN

p. 134, "We had a quiet township . . ." Swift, Samuel, op. cit., p. 192; p. 135, Buildings at Middlebury. Ibid., p. 298; p. 136, Graham's appraisal of Painter. Graham, J. A. *Descriptive Sketch of the Present State of Vermont. One of the United States of America.* London, 1797. p. 128; p. 137, Letter to Davis. *Land Records*, Vol. 1, p. 35. Ms. Plainfield Town Clerk's Office; "South on Orange . . ." Ibid., p. 29; p. 138, Law on Mills. *Laws of the State of Vermont* 1788, p. 407; p. 139, Ebenezer Markham. Swift, Samuel. op. cit., p. 289; Annexation of Cornwall. Matthews, Lyman. *History of Cornwall, Vermont*, p. 131; pp. 141, 142, Law on Inns. *Acts and Laws of the State of Vermont* 1799, pp. 24-30; p. 143, Common. Swift, Samuel. op. cit., p. 21; p. 145, Samuel's letter. Ms. Mar. 15, 1797. Sheldon Museum; p. 146, Victoria's letter. Ms. To Mrs. Hannah Keep Sheldon, July 30, 1797. Sheldon Museum; pp. 146 ff. Painter's letter. Ms. To Moses Sheldon, July 6, 1797. Sheldon Museum.

CHAPTER EIGHT

p. 153, "The influence of Painter . . ." Swift, Samuel, op. cit., p. 244; pp. 153, 154, Addison County Grammer School enactment. *Acts and Laws—State of Vermont* 1797, pp. 36-38; p. 157, Dwight's comment on College. Dwight, Timothy. *Travels in New England and New York*, Vol. II, pp. 415, 416; p. 158, "Petition of Gamaliel Painter," *Journals of the General Assembly* 1798, p. 205; pp. 158, 159, Assembly minutes. op. cit., 1708, p. 262; p. 159, "Committee of seven." op. cit., 1799, p. 12; pp. 159, 160, Committee report. Ibid., p. 145; p. 160, Dwight's comment. Dwight, Timothy. op. cit., pp. 415, 416; p. 161, Paine College. *State Papers of Vermont*, Vol. III (3) p. 184; "laudable and generous donations." Ibid., Vol. III (4) p. 15; "to take measures." Ibid., p. 136; p. 162, Chipman's impeachment. *Journals of the General Assembly* 1800, p. 30; Committee report on College. op. cit., p. 177; p. 163, Resolution. op. cit., p. 183; Bill for college. op. cit., p. 204; pp. 163, 164, College Charter. *Acts and Laws—State of Vermont* 1800, pp. 36-40; p. 166, Ira Allen's letter to Painter. Ms. April 11, 1805, Vermont Historical Society; Ira H. Allen's letter to his

REFERENCE SOURCES

father. Wilbur, James. *Ira Allen*, Vol. II, p. 386; p. 167, College rules. *Middlebury College Corporation Records*. Ms. College Treasurer's Office.

CHAPTER NINE

p. 171, Parmelee's term. Swift, Samuel, op. cit., p. 404; pp. 172, 173, Mason's sermon. Mason, Thomas. *A Sermon Delivered at Middlebury, Vermont, on Occasion of the Anniversary Thanksgiving 1798*, Rutland 1799. Sheldon Museum; pp. 173, 174, Statute on town meetinghouses. *Laws of the State of Vermont 1798*, pp. 474-479; p. 174, Declaration on religious opinion. *Acts and Laws of the State of Vermont 1801*, p. 18; p. 175, Committee on drawing church plans. Swift, Samuel. op. cit., p. 408; p 176, Burton's sermon Burton, Asa. *Sermon Delivered at the Ordination of the Rev. Thomas Abbott Merrill*, Middlebury 1806. Sheldon Museum; p. 178, Sunless creed. *Articles of Consociation, Adopted A.D. 1798 by The Congregational Churches of the Western Districts of Vermont and Parts Adjacent*. Poultney 1822. Middlebury College Library; pp. 179, 180, Merrill's Sermon. Merrill, Thomas. *Election Sermon* Middlebury, 1806; p. 181, Articles of Consociation. op. cit.; pp. 181, 182, Swift's ode. *The Adviser or Vermont Evangelical Magazine*, July 1809.

CHAPTER TEN

p. 184, Apologetic addition. Slade, William. *Vermont State Papers*, p. 450; p. 185, Chipman's comment. Ibid., pp. XVIII-XIX; Painter as Assembly representative. Painter represented the town of Salisbury in 1786 and 1787; Middlebury in the following years: 1788, 1789, 1790, 1791, 1792, 1793, 1796, 1801, 1803, 1805, 1809, 1810; p. 186, Constitution Sect. I, Chapter I. *Laws of the State of Vermont, 1798*, p. 47; p. 187, Governor's salary. *Journals of the General Assembly* 1801, p. 50; pp. 188, 189, Governor's address. Ibid. 1803, pp. 13-17; p. 190, Censor's report. Ibid. 1791, p. 26; Censor's report of 1813. Ibid. 1813, p. 42; p. 194, Report on Bank bills. Ibid.; p. 195 ff. Painter's votes. Ibid. 1786–1815; p. 197, Governor's remonstrance. Ibid., p. 46; Council as "watchmen." Ibid., p. 42; "Our political horizon . . ." Ibid., p. 45; pp. 200, 201, Recommendation on College. Ibid. 1814, pp. 123-124

CHAPTER ELEVEN

p. 206, Enactment on road to Troy. *Acts and Laws—State of Vermont 1800*, pp. 77, 78; p. 207, Fine for neglect of highway. Ibid. 1808, p. 458; p. 208, Damage in transit. Ibid., p. 452; pp. 209 ff., Center Turnpike. Ibid. 1800, pp. 45-52; p. 212, Contract for Center Turnpike. *Center Turnpike*, Vol. I Ms. Sheldon Museum; p. 213 ff., Waltham Turnpike. *Acts and Laws—State of Vermont 1805*, pp. 147-161.

CHAPTER TWELVE

p. 220, Dwight's description. Dwight, Timothy. op. cit., Vol. II, p. 419; pp. 220, 221, Hall's description. Thompson, Zadock. *Gazetteer of the State of Vermont*, pp. 179-182; p. 223, Description of Abby Victoria. *Memorial to Abby Victoria Painter*, Sheldon Museum; p. 224, Society for Suppression of Vice. *Columbian Patriot*, Middlebury, Mar. 8, 1815; p. 225, Advertisement of horses, *Vermont Mirror*, Middlebury, May 5, 1813; p. 226, Increase in President's Salary. *Middlebury College Corporation Records*. Ms. Aug. 21, 1811; Legislative Response. *Journals of the General Assembly*, 1815, p. 159; pp. 226, 227, College lottery. Ibid., p. 160; p. 227, Three corporation representatives. *Middlebury College Corporation Records*, Aug. 18, 1819; p. 229, Painter's guarantee. Ms. Sheldon Museum; Charitable Society. *Vermont Evangelical Magazine*, Sept. 1813; p. 230, Doggerel. *Philomathesian Society Records*, Aug. 18, 1807, Middlebury College Library; p. 231, Corporation Committees. *Middlebury College Corporation Records*, Oct. 1, 1810 and Nov. 10, 1812; p. 232, Abby Victoria's comments. *Memorial to Abby Victoria Painter*; pp. 233, 234, Will. *Land Records*. Ms. Town Clerk's Office, Middlebury; p. 234, Obituary notice. *National Standard*, May 26, 1819.

ABOUT THE AUTHOR

The greatest ovation to which Gamaliel Painter was ever subjected occurred not in Middlebury or Vermont but at Carnegie Hall in Manhattan during the winter of 1928 when the Middlebury College Glee Club, in competition with multiple New England college glee clubs voiced their favorite college songs. The Middlebury Club with its cane rappings and tappings in honor of Gamaliel, unequivically won first place, with thunderous and prolonged applause. Storrs Lee's tenor was one of the participant voices. Then and there he decided that Gamaliel deserved a biography as well as a song, though it took some twenty years to fulfill the resolve.

Like Painter, Mr. Lee migrated from Connecticut to Vermont. After graduation from college in 1928 and a year at Oxford University, he returned to Middlebury as instructor in the English Department and, with the title of College Editor, had responsibility for the editorship of all official monthly publications, including the quarterly alumni magazine. Quite appropriately he was assigned to an office in *Painter* Hall, and instead of a modern edifice, he chose to erect a home that belonged to Painter's generation; on a hillside a mile west of the college, overlooking a 75-mile reach of the Green Mountains, he built for his family a log house that became the site of many college festivities, as well as a stage for his wife, Mary Louise, an exponent of Modern Dance.

In addition to the editing of College publications, Mr. Lee soon became involved in a variety of town affairs. As trustee of the local Sheldon Museum, he was largely responsible for its conversion from a disorganized town attic into a popular museum, later serving for ten years as its president. In 1936 his history of Middlebury College, *Father Went to College*, was widely reviewed and used as the subject of newspaper features. In 1941, during the absence of Dr. Paul D. Moody, he served as college President with two other faculty members. Summoned to active duty as a Naval Reserve Intelligence officer later that year, he spent most of the World War II period in the Pacific area, where he attained the rank of Commander.

Upon his release from Naval Service, he returned to Middlebury as Dean of Men for a period of ten years, during which he found time to draft his biography of Gamaliel Painter. Following his departure from Middlebury he established summer headquarters at Pemaquid Point in Maine and winter·headquarters first in Berkeley, California, and later in Hawaii.

His first volume composed during this period, *Yankees of Connecticut*, won its author life membership in the elite Society of American Historians. His account of the Panama Canal construction, *The Strength to Move a Mountain*, brought commendation from both Houses of Congress, and a British edition was also published in London. Quite unintentionally, so far as the author was concerned, his volume on college deaning, *God Bless Our Queer Old Dean*, was adopted as a text for college classes in educational administration, but a book on Hawaii, *The Islands*, became his best seller. In 1969 he was the recipient of the Seattle Historical Society Award for his book *Washington State: A Literary Chronicle*. Invited to edit a series on other states, he completed only five before retirement in Maine. Altogether he is the author or editor of two dozen books.

INDEX

academy, chartered as County Grammar School, 153-154; chartered as Middlebury College, 156, 157-163; expanded into Middlebury College, 156; financing, 154; first building, 154-155; its first principal, 155-156; land donated, 152-153

Addison County, in 1785, 97-99; legal profession, 120-121; named for Joseph Addison, 98

Addison County courthouse, construction, 142-144; siting, 117, 123

Allen College, proposed, 151

Allen, Ethan, 18; commands Green Mountain Boys, 25-28; defeat of Fort Ticonderoga, 31-36; his fate, 39-40; and Green Mountain Boys, 25-29, 31-38; and guerrilla warfare, 7; and independent attempt on Canada, 39-40; and pre-Revolution turmoil, 15; property quarrels, 18, 103-104; raid on Panton, 25-29; scheme to found own community, 128

Allen, Ira, as Gamaliel Painter's partner, 127, 136-137; investing in Winooski Valley, 109; relinquishes interest in University of Vermont, 166; sends sons to Middlebury College, 166

Arnold, Benedict, and Elisha Painter's court martial, 68; exposure as traitor, 71-72; Gamaliel Painter's plea to, 70-72; Lake Champlain, 31-38; raid into Canada, 37-38; taking of Crown Point, 37

Artificers, at the Battle of Monmouth, 63; described, 55-56, 57-62, 65-66; deteriorating conditions, 75; discharged, 75-76; and Elisha Painter, 54-55, 60-68; Gamaliel Painter's service, 55-77, 205; their pay, 66, 69-72; regiment in Continental Army, 55

Atwater, Jeremiah, admission examiner, 165; College presidency, 157, 201; first principal of the academy, 155-156; protégé of Timothy Dwight, 156

Baldwin, Jeduthan, 49, 57; and Gamaliel Painter, 55; military engineer in Revolution, 42-44, 49

Barnett, John, ordained as pastor, 171-172

Battle of Monmouth, 61-63

Beach, Sam, 31-32

Bennington, 4, 15, 17, 98

Bill of Rights, Vermont's violation, 173-174

border disputes, 18, 22, 15-23, 25-29, 40-51, 128-129

Bread Loaf road, 209-210

Brewster, Oliver, Middlebury tailor, 136

bridge, at Middlebury Falls, 105-107, 140-141

Canada, and its incursion via Lake Champlain, 45; proposed conquest of, 196-197, 199-200; raided in Revolution, 37-38, 39-43

center of Town of Middlebury, church building, 182; at Gamaliel Painter's home, 92, 231;

siting church, 117, 170

Center Turnpike Company, 210

Champlain Valley, early settlers, 3-23; pillage after fall of Fort Ticonderoga, 51

Chipman, Abigail, marries Gamaliel Painter, 13

Chipman, Daniel, and charter for County Grammar School, 153-154, 157-158; criticizes state legislature, 185; Middlebury lawyer, 121; support for Grammar School, 157-158; and turnpikes, 210, 213

Chipman, John, 11, 12, 14; ambition, 84; his barn in Middlebury, 79; church services, 171; cited for overcharging, 162; founding Town of Middlebury, 11, 12-14, 16, 17, 18, 19, 20; Gamaliel Painter marries John.s sister Abigail, 13-15; Gamaliel Painter's partner, 141-142; and Green Mountain Boys, 26, 33; his marriage, 14; and Middlebury famine, 125; his Middlebury grant, 12-13, 14-18, 19-23; as pastor, 115; and siting of Middlebury church, 128

Chipman, Samuel, member of Vermont bar, 121

Chittenden County, carved from Addison County, 116

church, building, 176-182; Congregational vs. Episcopal, 174-175; Foot's barn, 115, 170; establishment in Middlebury, 127-128, 144, 170-177, 180-183; financed by sale of pews, 177; fund raising, 170, 181; influence, in Middlebury, 113, 117; and John Chipman, 171; location, 127-128, 142, 144, 170, 172, 173, 174-175; Middlebury's need for, 114-115, 122-123, 170; and Stephen Goodrich, 171; and Ebenezer Sumner, 171; taxing of congregation, 173-174; and Will Thayer, 171

Constitution of Vermont, convention, 49-51; and Gamaliel Painter, 185-186

Continental Army, standards of conduct, 59-60

Continental Congress, 39

Cornwall, 39; controversy with Town of Middlebury, 94-95; Gamaliel Painter elected to office, 109; Gamaliel Painter owns property there, 81; merger with Middlebury, 140-141; multiple towns, 4-5

Davis, Jacob, and Gamaliel Painter's land dealings, 137

Declaration of Independence, 45-46

Deming, John, blacksmith and first tavern-keeper in Middlebury, 135; Gamaliel Painter's partner, 141

distillery, established in Middlebury, 134

Doolittle, Joel, 175

Dorset convention, in Vermont legal history, 185

Dwight, Timothy, approval of Middlebury College, 156-157; concern over University of Vermont, 160; and Seth Storrs, 139; visits Middlebury, 156, 220

Emma Willard Seminary, 223
Everts, John, 4-5, 8, 10, 11; founding Town of
    Middlebury, 4-5; inaccurate survey, 90-91, 93

famine, in Middlebury, 124-126
farming, in Middlebury, 85-88, 89
fees, at Middlebury College, 201
Fillmore, Lavius, church architect, 176-177
Fishkill (New York), as army encampment, 64,
    66, 70-72, 73-76
Foot, Daniel, bridge at Middlebury Falls, 106-
    107; his barn, 115-116, 143, 170; bridge, 105-
    107; church establishment, 115; and church
    services, 170; competition with Gamaliel
    Painter's mills, 101, 139; controversy with
    Gamaliel Painter, 85, 94-95, 103; donates land
    for academy, 153; in early Middlebury, 85; fine
    for obstructing highway, 116; Gamaliel
    Painter's social festivities, 110; mill at
    Middlebury Falls, 101, 103, 133; 105-107; and
    siting of Middlebury church, 128
Fort Ticonderoga, and Green Mountain Boys, 31-
    37; loss of to the British, 49-50, 51; the struggle
    for, 31-51, passim; taking by Green Mountain
    Boys, 32-37
Fuller, Josiah, Middlebury tanner, 136
fund raising, church, 170, 181; and lottery, 207;
    for Middlebury College, 225-228; a pastor's
    salary, 171

Goodrich, Stephen, and church services, 171
Goodrich, William, and Gamaliel Painter's mills,
    138
Gorton, Benjamin, Middlebury storekeeper, 134
Graham, John, and Gamaliel Painter, 136;
    Middlebury lawyer, 121
Green Mountain Boys, 22-23, 25-28; border dis-
    putes, 128; after the Declaration of
    Independence, 44-45, 51; Elisha Painter's
    rejection by, 54-55; and Ethan Allen, 25-38;
    fall of Fort Ticonderoga, 31-37; Gamaliel
    Painter, 25-51; informal organization, 59; local
    terrorism, 31, 46-47; Panton Raid, 26-28; prop-
    erty disputes, 25; raid into Canada, 37-38, 39-
    40; as regular regiment, 39-51; and Revolution
    in Champlain Valley, 26-51; as state legislators,
    183
Green Mountain range, as boundary of Addison
    County, 116
Green Mountain Boys, 39; Canada raid, 40-43
guerrilla warfare, 25-29
gun factory, 139

Hall, Erastus, Middlebury saddler, 136
Hand's Cove, and assault on Fort Ticonderoga,
    32, 33
Hill, Festus, Middlebury carpenter, 136
Hooker, Thomas, ix
horses, Gamaliel Painter as breeder, 225

judgeship, Gamaliel Painter's, 113-114, 116-123,
    128, 129, 193, 196; justice of the peace, 107,
    108; side judge, 99, 114

Lake Champlain, as boundary of Addison
    County, 116; first bridge, 43, 49; in
    Revolution, 44-51
Lake Dunmore, as boundary of Addison County,
    116
law and order, in Middlebury, 113
Lee, Charles, defects at Battle of Monmouth, 62
legal profession, in Addison County, 120-123
legislation, in Vermont, 186-196
legislature, and Gamaliel Painter, 181-201; infor-
    mal character of, 181-185
lottery, and fund raising, 207, 226-227

marble industry, in Middlebury, 221
Markham, Ebenezer, first nail factory in
    Vermont, 139
Mason, Thomas, pastor, 172-173
Mathews, Darius, donates land for academy, 153;
    practicing medicine in Middlebury, 135
Mattocks, Sam, Middlebury tavern keeper, 136
merger, of Cornwall and Middlebury, 140-141
Merrill, Thomas, pastor, 169, 175-176, 178-180
Middlebury College, academy, 154; Addison
    County Grammar School, 153-154; admission
    of first class, 165; Atwater resigns presidency,
    201; bequest of Gamaliel Painter, 233-234;
    Board of Trustees, 225, 231; County Grammar
    School, 153-154; endowment, 229; endows
    Painter professorship, 234; fees, 201; first
    trustees, 164-165; Gamaliel Painter as fund rais-
    er, 225-228, 231; influence of religion, 220; pro-
    posed merger with University of Vermont, 227;
    siting problems, 228; state support for, 200-201;
    student aid, 229; students at church, 179-180
Middlebury Falls, also known as Painter's Falls,
    136; bridge, 106; center of town, 92-94, 100-
    101, 111, 132-133, 135; courthouse location,
    117, 123, 142-144; Daniel Foot's mill, 101,
    103; Gamaliel Painter's mill, 101-103; settle-
    ment, 93-94
Miller, Samuel, and charter for County Grammar
    School, 153-154; expansion of academy, 154;
    Middlebury lawyer, 121, 135; and turnpikes,
    210

nail factory, 139
New Hampshire, chartering of towns, 5-7
New Hampshire Grants, 4-11, 13, 22, 25, 28, 29,
    30-31, 41, 40, 46; bid for autonomy, 47; border
    disputes, 46-47; guerrilla warfare, 25-29; and
    Revolution, 44; Vermont's split-off, 4-23
New Haven, multiple towns, 4-5
New York, claim to Vermont, 22-23, 25, 29
Nicholas, Jonathan, and industry in Cornwall,
    139

248

Nicholas, Josiah, and industry in Cornwall, 139

old families, Ackley, 83; Allen, 7, 11, 15, 18, 19, 25-28, 32-40, 44, 54, 59, 103-104, 108, 127, 136-137; Atwater, 157; Barnett, 171-172; Beach, 31-32; Bentley, 22; Blodgett, 93; Brewster, 136; Brush, 118; Buell, 16; Chandler, 80, 86; Chipman, 11, 12-14, 15, 16, 17, 18, 19-23, 26, 33, 79, 80, 84, 92, 110, 115, 118, 121, C125, 128, 141-142. 153-154, 157-158, 162, 164, 171, 174-175, 185, 210, 213; Davis, 137; Deming, 118, 125, 135, 141-142; Doolittle, 175; Dudley, 103, 105, 108, 110; Everet, 118; Everts, 4-5, 8, 10, 11, 80, 84, 90; Foot, 85, 94-95, 101, 103, 105-107, 110, 115, 116, 128, 139, 153, 170, 172; Freeman, 110; Fuller, 136; Goodrich, 85, 110, 138, 152, 171; Gorton, 134; Graham, 121, 136; Hagar, 175; Hall, 118, 119, 136; Hill, 136; Hinman, 84; Holbrook, 104; Hyde, 22, 79, 82; Johnson, 93, 110; Jones, 104-105; Kirby, 83; Knox, 57; Markham, 139. Mason, 172-173; Mathews, 135, 152-153, 156; Mattocks, 136, 118, 172, 210; Merrill, 169; Miller, 121, 135, 156-157, 210; Morley, 113; Moulton, 39; Munger, 83. 110; Nicholas, 139; Owen, 22; Paine, 161; Perigo, 103; Perkins, 86-87, 124; Preston, 110; Reed, 4-5; Reid, 26, Rhodes, 153; Risley, 85; Rogers, 134, 135; Selleck, 83; Seymour, 175; Slasson, 22, 85; Sloan, 84; Smalley, 22, 84-85; Southworth, 152; Spaulding, 14; Spencer, 46-47; Stillman, 110; Storrs, 110, 139, 121,139, 152-153, 156, 165, 210; Story, 84; Sumner, 110, 171; Thayer, 79, 82, 171; Tillotson, 86, 110; Torrance, 79, 82, 84, 89; Tupper, 83; Wadsworth, 110; Warner, 38, 39, 41, 43, 44, 45, 46, 51, 54, 55, 59, 60; Washburn, 14, 80, 92, 94. 101-102, 110; Wilder, 136; Willard, 136, 175; Wyman, 136; Young, 134

Olin, Henry, Middlebury lawyer, 121

Otter Creek, 5, 6, 12, 17, 21. 26. 28, 39, 85, 91, 92, 93; Abigail Painter's funeral procession, 126-127; flooding, 101-102; obstacle to road-building, 205

Paine, Elijah, siting of proposed Allen college, 161
Paine College, an aborted proposal, 160-161
Painter, Abby Victoria, 223-224
Painter, Abigail, death of, 126-127
Painter, Elisha, 7, 9, 11, 12, 131, 20, 40; court-martialed, 66-68; death of, 68; Gamaliel's brother, 7-9; and Green Mountain Boys, 38, 45; incompatibility with Gamaliel, 53-55; officer in Continental Regiment, 44-45; sells town of Middlebury stake, 11
Painter, Gamaliel, Addison County judgeship, 99, 108-109; 113-114, 116-123, 128, 129, 193, 196; Addison County sheriff, 99-100; ancestry, 8; and Artificers, 44, 55, 69-77; at Battle of

Monmouth, 63; bequeaths estate to Middlebury College, 233-234; blacksmith, 81; breeds horses, 225; his brother Elisha, 55; builder of public works, 217; builds his house, 108-111, 126; 145-149, 170; Center Turnpike Company presidency, 212-217; and charter for County Grammar School, 153-154; church efforts, 127-128, 176-182; cobbler, 12, 81; collapse of his property rights, 11, 90-91; commercial success, 141-142; Connecticut connections, 51, 57, 81; Continental Army, 53-54, 81; controversy with Daniel Foot, 85, 94-95, 103, 106, 128, 139; cooperates on bridge with Daniel Foot, 105-107; his daughter, Abby Victoria, 145, 222-224, 231-233; death of Gamaliel, 234-235; death of his second wife, Victoria, 177-178; death of his son Joseph, 177; death of his son Samuel, 145-149; education, 151-152; elected to office by Cornwall, 109; endows Middlebury College, 229-230; engineer, 81; establishment of Town of Middlebury center, 100-101, 131-133-144; farmer, 12, 13, 14, 16, 19-21, 29-30, 81, 86-89, 95; first marriage, to Abigail Chipman, 13; Green Mountain Boys, 25-31, 51; and idea for academy, 152-153; manufacturer, 81; master carpenter, 57-59, 61; membership in Middlebury organizations, 224-225; and Middlebury College regulations, 166-167; and Middlebury College student aid, 229; miller, 102, 108; his mills, 92, 101-103, 107, 127, 133, 137-141, 148-149, 177; moderator, 108; his move to Middlebury, 7-8, 10-11, 12-23; multiple trades, 12; in a nutshell, x-xii; oath of allegiance to United States, 61-62; offers his home for Middlebury College trustees' meetings, 231; partner with Ira Allen, 136-137; pastoral duties, 114; peacemaker, 108; prominence in post-Revolution Middlebury, 81-89, 95; public offices, 107-109; public service, 130-132; prosperity, 127; and real estate dealings, 11, 81-82, 102, 108, 121, 127, 132-137; and religion, 169, 224; and Revolution, 29-51; and search for pastor, 127-128; second marriage, to Victoria, 144-145; sells home farm in Connecticut, 15-16; setting center of Town of Middlebury, 102, 107, 108, 109-111, 135-136; settlement of Middlebury Falls area, 92-94; shopkeeper, 81; siting of Town of Middlebury, 219-220; state legislature, 107-108; 183-201; supervisor of military construction, 43-44; 144-145, 146; as surveyor, 12, 81, 90, 92-93, 108, 127; Surveyor of Highways, 203-217; tanner, 12; tavern keeper, 141-142; third marriage, 222; title to Middlebury property, 18-19, 22-23, 46; and turnpike business, 209-216; and Vermont constitution, 49-51, 185-186; and Vermont establishment, 45-47, 49, 50-51; and Vermont's statehood, 129; and Winooski Valley Land, 224; wartime spy, 48-49; welcome in Addison County towns, 91

Painter, William, and lumber, 138-139
Painter Hall, construction of, 228-229
Painter's Falls, also known as Middlebury Falls, 135-136
Panton Raid, 26-28
pastor, controversy over recruiting, 171; John Barnett, 171-172; John Chipman, 115; Gamaliel Painter as quasi-pastor, 114; salary problems, 171; Thomas Mason, 169, 172, 175-176, 178-180; Thomas Merrill, 169, 175-176, 178-180
Perkins, Nathan, and famine in Middlebury, 124-126
potash production, 134, 140

Reed, Elias, role in founding Town of Middlebury, 4-5
religion, Gamaliel Painter forms religious society, 224; in Gamaliel Painter's life, 169-182, 220; influence on Middlebury College, revival furor, 223-224
Revolution, 44-51; and the Champlain Valley, 30-51
Rhodes, Anthony, donates land for academy, 153
Ripton Gap, 209-210
roads, construction and maintenance, 203-209; financing by taxes, 216; private turnpikes, 209-216
Rogers, Jabez, inventories buildings in Middlebury, 135; storekeeper and distiller, 134

Salisbury, Gamaliel Painter represents town in State legislature, 106, 108; multiple towns, 4-5
Seymour, Horatio, and Episcopal church, 175
sheep, in Middlebury, 88-89
site of Town of Middlebury, chosen by Painter, 219-22
siting, controversy over a college in Vermont, 160-161; of Middlebury College building, 228
Spencer, Benjamin, leader in border disputes, 46-47
State legislature, Gamaliel Painter's election to, 107-108; meets in Middlebury, 161-162
statehood, Vermont achieves, 129
Storrs, Seth, 110; his career, 121, 139; donates land for academy, 152-153; and idea for academy, 152-153; property-owner in Cornwall, 139; and turnpikes, 210
Sumner, Ebenezer, and church services, 171

tannery, 140
taverns, 8, 10, 15, 39, 83, 93, 110, 118, 139, 141-142
taxation, 204-206, 207, 209; for church building, 173-174; for roads and bridges, 106, 203-209; school, 154; tea tax and Revolution, 15
Thayer, Will, and church services, 171

Tichenor, Isaac, issues College charter, 163-164
Town of Middlebury, access to, 205-206; its center, 101-102; chartering, 5-7; church services, 113, 114-115, 117. 123, 127-128, 122-123, 142, 144, 170, 173, 174-175; 176-182; ; controversy with Town of Cornwall, 94-95; development, 131-144, 220-221; early times, 11-16, 22-23, 29-30; establishment of a church, 114, 127-128, 144, 170-177; famine, 123-127; farm foundations, 85; its first charter, 5-7; its first store, 134; first town meeting, 5-11; founder, x; Gamaliel Painter's devotion to, 44, 45, 91, 234-235; growth of, 219-221; in 1800, 161-162; incorrectly surveyed, 90; lumber, 138-139; marble industry, 221; merger with Cornwall, 140-141; Middlebury Falls, 100; multiple towns, 4-5; its people described, 86-88; post-Revolution desolation, 79-81; professions, 135-144; regeneration after Revolutionary War, 82-89; social season, 109-110; its water power, 92-95, 131-133 turnpikes, the Waltham Turnpike, 213-217

University of Vermont, x-xi; competitor of Middlebury College, 160-161, 162-164, 165-166; proposed merger with Middlebury College, 227

Vermont, admission to the Union, 128-129
Vermont, border disputes, 128-129; its constitutional convention, 49-51; establishment as separate state, 47; shifting borders, 97; state university, 127
Vermont economy, and self-sufficiency, 125-126

Waltham Turnpike, 213-217
Warner, Seth, 41, 46; defeat at Hubbardton, 51; and Elisha Painter, 54; and Green Mountain Rangers, 39
Washington, George, and Artificers in Continental Army, 56, 57, 61, 65-66, 72, 75-77; Battle of Monmouth, 62-63; demands for better military pay, 56, 66, 72-73; Elisha Painter's court martial, 67; Valley Forge, 61; signs Act creating State of Vermont, 129
water power, and siting of towns, 92, 131
water rights, sale of, 177
Wilder, Elias, Middlebury hatter, 136
Willard, John, Middlebury doctor, 136
Williams, Roger, ix
Windsor convention, in Vermont legal history, 185
Winooski Valley, 104; Gamaliel Painter sells his land, 136-137, 224; Painter's investment, 108, 127
Winthrop, John, 8
Wyman, Daniel, Middlebury lawyer, 136

Young, William, Middlebury cabinetmaker, 134